ROUGHING IT FOR CHRIST IN THE WILDS OF BRAZIL

ABRINDO FRONTEIRAS PARA CRISTO NAS SELVAS DO BRASIL

ABRIENDO FRONTERAS PARA CRISTO EN LAS SELVAS DE BRASIL

Roughing It for Christ in the Wilds of Brazil

Abrindo Fronteiras para Cristo nas Selvas do Brasil

Abriendo fronteras para Cristo en las selvas de Brasil

Albert Lehenbauer

The Phyllis E. Buehner Duesenberg
History of Lutheran Missions Book Series

CONCORDIA PUBLISHING HOUSE • SAINT LOUIS

The Concordia Historical Institute Monograph Series exists to publish and disseminate significant and engaging research connected with the history of the confessional Lutheran Church in North America, especially that historical research making use of the material held by the archive and library of Concordia Historical Institute, as well as material held by the archives and libraries of other entities of The Lutheran Church—Missouri Synod.

PREVIOUS VOLUMES

Seminex in Print: A Comprehensive Bibliography of Published Material and Selected Archival Resources for Historical Research. Compiled by David O. Berger with Daniel N. Harmelink (2021).

The Emigration of the Saxon Lutherans in the Year 1838 and Their Settlement in Perry County, Missouri by J. F. Koestering. Translated by Brian Lutz and G. H. Naumann. Revised for publication by Matthew Carver (2022).

Rediscovering the Issues Surrounding the 1974 Concordia Seminary Walkout. Edited by Ken Schurb (2023).

A Hundredfold Harvest: A Survey of Mission Work in Travancore, South India, in the Early 1900s. Heinrich Nau. Translated by Matthew Carver (2025).

Published by Concordia Publishing House
3558 S. Jefferson Ave., St. Louis, MO 63118-3968
1-800-325-3040 • cph.org

Originally published as *Roughing It for Christ in the Wilds of Brazil*, Zwickau: Johannes Herrmann, 1923.

Manufactured in the United States of America

1 2 3 4 5 6 7 8 9 10 35 34 33 32 31 30 29 28 27 26

Contents • Conteúdo • Contenido

In Memoriam

Phyllis E. Buehner Duesenberg
(February 20, 1933–June 12, 2019)

Member of the Concordia Historical Institute Board of Governors
(November 2008–June 2019)

This volume / collection made possible by the
Phyllis E. Buehner Duesenberg History of Lutheran Missions Fund

Roughing It for Christ in the Wilds of Brazil

[Jesus said,] "Ye shall be My witnesses . . . unto the uttermost part of the earth." (Acts 1:8)

Albert Ernst Heinrich Lehenbauer

ALBERT ERNST HEINRICH LEHENBAUER

(FEBRUARY 13, 1891–APRIL 29, 1955)

REV. ALBERT E. H. LEHENBAUER WAS BORN in West Ely, Missouri, on February 13, 1891, the eighth child of Conrad and Catherine (Preusser) Lehenbauer's nine children. His father died when he was five years old, and from then on his mother made sure that, after his confirmation on Palm Sunday (in 1905 by Pastor Pflanz), he would continue his education and enter the seminary in St. Louis. He graduated from Concordia Seminary in 1913. Albert very much aspired to enter the foreign mission field and serve as a missionary in China. However, before leaving his native land for the East, he decided to wait a year. With the beginning of the Great War in 1917, it was no longer possible to send missionaries to China. This caused Albert to accept a call to Brazil instead, where both of his brothers—Conrad (who served as pastor in Arroio do Meio) and George (who served as pastor in Santa Cruz)—had previously been sent.

Albert Lehenbauer arrived in Porto Alegre in 1915, on Dia dos Navegantes (a holiday in Porto Alegre celebrated every February 2). Because he did not speak Portuguese, and all commerce was closed, after several attempts he was able to locate the Lutheran seminary. After visiting his two brothers for a short time, Albert traveled via train to Ijuí, where Pastor E. Miller was waiting for his arrival. From there, they traveled by horse and buggy to Linha 23, and then to Guarany, his new residence. His first sermon in April of that same year was based on St. Luke 18:9–14, a passage that so very clearly describes God's grace and love. About this same grace and love of God, Albert preached, taught, and wrote during all his years in the ministry, being a great example to his congregants located in thirteen mission stations, including his home in Linha 15, which he affectionately called Urwahnfried ("Fullfillment"). This was precisely why he began youth meetings with young men he believed to be good candidates for the pastoral ministry, teaching them the Christian doctrines on Sunday nights whenever possible.

Because he believed in the importance of good reading materials for Christian education, Albert Lehenbauer was the first editor of the annual directory entitled Luther-Kalender. He also wrote a great number of articles for the Kirchenblatt, the Leitor Brasileiro, and other periodicals within and outside Brazil. His clear and simple way of writing reflected his faith in the teachings of the Bible and the writings of Martin Luther.

Because of his many and varied God-given gifts, he was soon elected to be a member of the Mission Committee, and shortly afterward he was elected to be the director of the Mission Department for all of Brazil. In addition, he served as vice president of the "Book of Concord" Lutheran church body of Brazil from 1928 to 1932. He was required to do much traveling to carry out his responsibilities—not just in the state of Rio Grande do Sul but also abroad.

On December 31, 1918, Albert Lehenbauer married Helena Priebe. Six of their eight children were born in Brazil at Urwahnfried. Their second son, Reginald, was born in Hannibal, Missouri, in 1923, while the family was on sabbatical leave in the United States. At the end of his sabbatical year, Albert and Helena and their two sons returned to Brazil and arrived in Urwahnfried on November 12, 1923. Their youngest son was born in Argentina in 1939.

Previously, Albert had noticed that in certain places where his church members had planted various grains, each passing year the exhausted soil produced less and less. Therefore he began to research this problem in the hopes of finding a solution. Being an avid reader, Albert eventually discovered an article that explained how certain plants (legumes) add nitrogen to the soil, a natural fertilizer. Better yet, these plants grow where other plants can no longer do so. Upon learning that the soybean is one of these nitrogen-producing plants, he was convinced that planting soybeans would be a good solution for the problem his church members were facing. That being the case, on his return from his sabbatical, he brought back to Brazil a bottle with a handful of soybean seeds from his parents' farm in Missouri.

No sooner after arriving home at Urwahnfried, Albert jumped off the buggy and planted the seeds in their garden. In 1924, as he harvested what the first seeds produced, he kept half of them and distributed the rest in small matchboxes containing two to three seeds to each of his parishioners with the instructions: "Plant these, and when they produce next year, give half away to a neighbor or friend, and tell them to do the same with their first harvest." (Albert also followed these guidelines and continued to distribute seeds after subsequent harvests.)

After a few harvests, the seeds began to multiply to such an extent that there were several people who reported that a single stock could produce four hundred pods. In an article he wrote later, Albert urges farmers to plant soybeans because of the great return and its varied culinary uses.

Farmers who planted soybeans found that in a short time they had much seed, and yet had little or no idea what to do with it. First, they tried to roast and mill the seeds, and then make a sort of coffee beverage, but the soy gummed up their coffee grinders, and when hot water was poured over the soybean powder, it produced a heavy layer of oil, making the hot beverage undrinkable.

Others tried to use soybean powder to make bread, which was not altogether bad as soon as it was taken out of the oven. However, after several hours, the loaf exuded oil and became unappetizing. Attempts at making soybean bread were therefore abandoned.

Finally, not knowing what to do with the soybeans and not wanting to question the good intentions of their pastor, one of the farmers decided to give the seeds to their pigs. In a short while, this caused a veritable revolution in the state's pork industry. Not only did the pigs grow more rapidly, but they also grew fatter. The same also happened when the farmers fed soybeans to their cows grown for milk and meat. Eventually, the soybean began to be used for making cooking oil, and what was left from this process became the principal feed for pigs and cows. From then on, the planting and harvesting of soybeans was a guaranteed success.

Today, Brazil is the second-largest producer of soybeans, with Argentina being the third. Brazil's production and export of soybeans and soy products continue to grow rapidly. Without doubt, this humble seed changed the lives of the Urwahnfried farmers in the state of Rio Grande do Sul, as well as farmers living in other states of Brazil and in Argentina and Paraguay. Today, soybeans are used in a large number of food and nonfood products.

In the first months of 1937, after serving as pastor and missionary in Brazil for twenty-two years, Pastor Albert Lehenbauer accepted a call to Argentina to be director of a pre-theological school (Concordia College). At that time, Argentina did not have a seminary. This meant that seminary students in Argentina had to relocate to the Lutheran seminary in Brazil or travel to the United States. However, the church was very interested in calling somebody to work in a preparatory school that would train future pastors in the Spanish language. The idea was to form pastors who could speak Spanish in order to supply the Argentinian church (and later other Spanish-speaking nations in South America as well). This school was started in Villa Crespo, and Albert served as its president from 1937 until 1942. In 1942, when he traveled to the United States, Pastor Lehenbauer convinced the Mission Department of The Lutheran Church—Missouri Synod of the necessity to help build a seminary in Argentina. Albert was the first director after Concordia Seminary was built in Villa Ballester, outside of Buenos Aires. He occupied this position from 1942 until 1946, when he transitioned to the position of theology professor at this seminary.

During his years of pastoral work in Argentina, Pastor Albert was also the co-editor of the Kirchengebote (1938–40), editor of the Evangelical Lutheran Hymnal (which also contained some hymns he had translated into Spanish), and he found time to coedit numerous books in Portuguese and Spanish during this period. He also wrote numerous papers presented at national conventions of the Brazilian and Argentinian churches.

In 1955, during the fifty-year jubilee, at the convention of the Lutheran Church of Argentina in Village San Juan, in the state of Entre Rios, Albert Lehenbauer was scheduled to do the closing devotion. This was to be his last official church function before his retirement. Shortly before boarding the train to return to Buenos Aires, he suffered from severe headaches. His two brothers, George and Conrad, and his two sons-in-law, Pastor Fernando Höhn and Pastor Edgar Kroger, were with him, as well as other church leaders. Even though his sons-in-law wanted to take him to the hospital, he thought it was better to go directly to Buenos Aires, thinking that all would soon pass. Because his headaches became much worse during the train ride, his sons-in-law moved him to the baggage wagon in order that he might lie down and be more comfortable. But when he realized that his condition was growing worse, he asked for his Bible and read the words of Psalm 23, and the verse from Psalm 119:105. Shortly after that, he could no longer speak intelligibly. Pastor R. Hasse joined the men as they ministered to Albert and asked him if he had faith in Jesus Christ. No longer able to respond with words, Albert did not hesitate to make a positive nod with his head. Even though he tried to communicate several more times, nobody could understand him. In a short time, he became unconscious and three days later, on April 29, 1955, died of a stroke at the hospital in Buenos Aires.

Albert's funeral was held at Concordia Seminary, Jose Leon Suarez, in the state of San Martin, Argentina. Three different sermons were preached during the services. President Rev. F. Lange preached in Spanish, Rev. S. H. Beckmann preached in German, and Rev. Dr. F. Hasse preached in Portuguese, while Rev. Ern. Hoapp officiated at the interment. Pastor Albert Lehenbauer was buried at the cemetery in the city of San Martin.

After Albert's death, Helena continued to live in their little house in Misiones, Argentina, for a number of years. In October 1970, she moved to New York City to live with her youngest daughter, Monica. Helena died February 17, 1986, and was buried next to her son, Reginald, in Fayetteville, North Carolina. Her grandson, Rev. Walter Lehenbauer, officiated at her interment.

Rev. Walter Lehenbauer
Cloquet, Minnesota

HISTORICAL INTRODUCTION

THE REV. ALBERT ERNST HEINRICH LEHENBAUER was born on February 13, 1891, in West Ely, Missouri (USA). He was sent by The Lutheran Church—Missouri Synod as a missionary to Brazil in 1914. He settled here in Santa Rosa (now Ubiretama), where he married Helena Priebe and had eight children. Together with local leaders, he founded the Colonial Union at Boundary Line July 23, where, in addition to studying the Word, he encouraged the cultivation of soybeans and other agricultural practices.

And this Pastor Albert Lehenbauer was an instrument of God, not only to maintain the faith of these Lutheran immigrants who needed spiritual assistance but also to improve the lives of farmers who lived with great difficulties, with few schools, and with few technical resources to work in the agricultural area.

So on one of his vacation trips, he decided to bring a handful of soybean seeds from the United States, which he distributed among the settlers who were taking part in his Bible studies. With this he not only found an alternative for the mere survival of the society around him but also found solutions, establishing an agricultural revolution. He became the most important agent of transformation in the city's history from 1924 onward. In addition to his faithful work as an LCMS missionary, pastor, and educator, he used his other qualifications in education and agriculture to serve his congregants.

Through his work in society, Pastor Albert became a leading figure in promoting the social well-being of the society in which he found himself. He was no mere spectator. He was a leader of transformation, inspiring new projects, strengthening partnerships, and creating a different kind of agriculture throughout the country. Through his actions, he was an instrument of change that has impacted the society to this day.

In November 2024, when the one hundredth anniversary of soybeans in Brazil was celebrated at the Fenasoja (National Soybean Fair) in Santa Rosa, this pastor was the main character in this beautiful story of mission and transformation.

Pastor Lehenbauer worked here in Brazil for twenty-three years. Then he accepted a call to Argentina, where he continued his mission!

Rev. Mario Lehenbauer, Pastor Emeritus
Evangelical Lutheran Church of Brazil

Roughing It for Christ in the Wilds of Brazil

IT WAS ABOUT EIGHT YEARS AGO that Rev. C. Trünow and [I] sailed from New York on the *S. S. Vasari*, bound for our respective mission fields in South America. He was going to the Argentine; I had a call to Brazil. The ocean trip to Rio de Janeiro, where we were to part, was a soft and sunny one. But after that I began to rough it. At the customs office, I found that I did not have half enough money to pay my duty. Luckily Mr. Trünow could lend me the necessary amount.

At the port of Santos, known for its coffee export, I was nearly left behind, owing to the fact that the sailing time of my steamer, a coast liner, had been advanced in my absence from the ship, without my knowledge or connivance. I spent my last paper money in hiring a rowboat. But I succeeded in overtaking the steamer. This action of the captain, which I considered a great piece of rudeness against my worthy person, made it impossible, for lack of funds, to buy any refreshments during the remaining four days of the trip. Oh, the fine bananas, oranges, coconuts, and pineapples that I couldn't buy! But that was no misfortune compared with what it would have been, if I had missed my steamer altogether.

There had been no opportunity to write nor money to wire the date of my arrival to the brothers in southern Brazil, and I knew there would be nobody to meet me at the dock. We landed at Porto Alegre, the capital of Rio Grande do Sul, which is the southernmost state of the Republic of Brazil, on a holiday, and I found most of the places of business closed. Our seminary was at that time concealed in an inconspicuous suburb, and I had a hard time getting any information in regard to it. Three times, and from three entirely different directions, I was sent to one and the same Catholic seminary. At noon, I lunched on the most delicious grapes, which I bought for my last coins (excepting enough for carfare) and by means of sign language, as I had not the least idea that in Portuguese, the language of the land, they bear the same name as in Latin: "uva." Nor did I know whether I was getting them by the pound, foot, or quire. At length, after lugging my hand baggage around for all of five hours, I did find a German who had once heard one of our professors preach and could tell me the way to our seminary.

After a few pleasant days among the brothers at Porto Alegre, I paid a short visit to each of my two brothers who had entered the Brazilian mission work within about a year before me. Then I boarded the wee train of the wee Brazilian railroad, bound for my own field. Guarany [Guarani] is its name, and by an unconscionable oversight of the mapmakers, it is not to be found on most maps. You won't find it on yours. For my part, I should prefer to have the North Pole omitted from the atlases, which is of no use whatever to anybody, while Guarany [Guarani] is to some people, me included, the center of the earth.

After two days of near seasickness on the narrow-gage and very much curvilinear and most shaky wee railroad, I arrived at Ijuhy [Ijuí], at that time the terminus of the [rail]road, where I was welcomed by Rev. Emil Müller. A distance of sixty miles still separated me from the terminus of my hopes and expectations, a stretch of unworked country roads that we were to conquer in a buggy that I had brought along for Rev. Müller. In consequence of heavy rains, the usual time of sixteen hours for this distance swelled into three full days. The first day took us along the nearly completed roadbed for the continuation of the wee railroad, to which I gleefully added the possessive pronoun of the first-person singular and called it "My Railroad." On the second and third days, my courage was kept up by Rev. Müller's assurance, which he cheerfully repeated ever so often: "Now, when we have conquered this hill before us, we shall be a good deal nearer than we are at present." This same reassurance served me well in my work later on when the road was very much uphill and muddy to boot.

Finally, we had climbed the last hill. We were at Guarany [Guarani]. Pronounce it "gwah-rah-nee," with a strong accent on the last syllable. This final "y" ["i"] in so many South American words is an Indian word for "water" or "river." But Guarany [Guarani] is at present not the name of a river but that of a large colonization conducted by the state government of Rio Grande do Sul. Of this large colony I was interested only in a small part, which is settled almost exclusively by German Russians. Try to imagine a huge piece of crumb cake about fifteen miles long and seven miles wide. The crumb part of the cake is pure, unbroken Brazilian forest primeval, consisting of trees with crooked trunks and a dense undergrowth of vines, shrubbery, bamboo, ferns, etc. Now imagine yourself cutting this cake lengthwise into strips 1-1/5-miles wide. I am sorry to burden your mind with these fractions, but they are caused by the fact that the metric system of weights and measures is used by the Brazilian government. I wish it were so in the United States too. Where the knife has passed in cutting the cake, we shall imagine bridle paths—in many places even closed at the top by the dense branches of the trees and the vines growing on them. Later on, these paths will be widened out into wagon and automobile roads, and a few of the most important ones could be used for wagon traffic when I arrived. Now, please, [make] one cut across the middle of the cake, converting each long strip into two shorter ones. This is our only crossroad; and a poor one at that, as most of the stumps seem to have chosen their places in the road and not beside it, and the one gutter or drainage ditch runs exactly down the center of the road. Now and then you meet a mudhole at the sight of which you feel uncertain whether to walk, swim, jump, or fly. As recently as 1921, I know of a case [in which] the horse of an immigrant suddenly and completely disappeared in such a hole and was barely saved from drowning. Your uncertainty is, however, not the hole's fault but is due to your inexperience. You are still a greenhorn in matters of Brazilian roads. You'll learn soon.

Now let us split each of our strips of cake into two narrower ones by a slit through the middle, which is not a road or path but merely a surveyor's line, and then cut them up entirely into bits a little more than half a mile long and 280-yards wide. These tracts, containing about sixty-two acres of forest land, are the "rural lots" or farms of the immigrants, sold to them on very easy terms by the state government at a price of about 125 U.S. dollars. As the immigrants were transported from their former homes to the spot by the Brazilian federal government besides, this wasn't a bad deal at all. Most of the farms had running water in the form of a spring, a brook, or a river.

When we speak of German Russians, we mean people of purely German extraction, who have, however, been inhabitants of Russia for one or more generations. In their more or less unmixed German colonies in Russia, they preserved most of the physical, mental, and cultural characteristics brought along from Germany one or more generations ago. In their language and customs, I am at times forcibly reminded of things that I read about German life about a hundred or more years back. This includes some very fine qualities and some that are bad. By some of them, but not by all, the propensity toward lying and stealing has been adopted from their Russian and Polish surroundings.

Nearly all of them are woodworkers in the most comprehensive sense of the term, being able to produce a remarkable variety of wooden articles with only the trees of the forest and a few simple tools at their service. I have seen them hew the longest sills, perfectly straight, without a chalk line. They saw their boards by hand with considerable speed and enjoy the work. They do the finest kind of wood polishing with very little apparatus and no ready-made rubbing varnishes. If ever anybody came easily by the land most suited to his particular needs, it was these German Russian immigrants to Brazil in the last ten years before the Great War [World War I]. I wish I could truthfully add that they are all grateful for it, and for the pleasant and healthful subtropical climate, and for having been spared the horrors of that world catastrophe.

In this crumb cake, settled by nearly [one] thousand families of immigrants, I was to take charge of my field for better or for worse. I took for granted that it was to be for better and rejoiced in the thought of the virgin forest, and the virgin soil in church and school affairs. But I was not long in finding out that I should have some sills to hew and some boards to saw in my missionary work. But why speak of mission work at all? Were these people heathens?

In name, they were Lutherans. But, in a majority of cases, their Lutheranism ended with the name and the baptismal and other certificates that they brought with them. The so-called Lutheran Church of Russia before the war suffered from all the diseases of the [union] state churches of Germany and had one or two special maladies of its own. It was not the worst of these that the pastors were sometimes forced to commune Lutherans in the Lutheran manner and members of the Reformed Church in their own way at the same altar. It was worse that the pastors were first and principally officials of the Russian government, having as their chief duty the keeping of the records that served as a basis for the military enlistments, and only in the second place shepherds of the flock of Christ. In most cases too, they were so overburdened with congregations that they rarely got to visit them more than once or twice a year, even though they did conduct two services on every day of the week while making their circuit. When they did come, they were so overrun with routine work that a pastor's chief work, the feeding of immortal souls with the preaching of the Word, could receive only a very minor part of their attention and of their physical powers. It was out of the question entirely for them personally to instruct their hundreds of catechumens. Many of these saw their pastor for the first time in their life on confirmation day. It is very doubtful whether on the average the pastor was personally acquainted with even as much as 1 percent of his parishioners either at the time of confirmation or in life after.

The usual Sunday service consisted in the reading of a sermon by a so-called teacher, who also took the place of the pastor in the instruction of the young and in most of the real pastoral work in most of the congregations. Most of these teachers had no training whatever, were unable to expound the chief doctrines of the Christian faith, and were usually content with having their catechumens memorize the chief parts of [the] catechism in a more or less faulty manner. Far from writing any books themselves, the pastors did not even supply the want of Lutheran books by importing them from Germany or America. The book supply was left in the hands of the Jews. It is true that there was little interest in good books. But were not the pastors the very persons that should have created this interest, and would it not have grown if only the supply had been taken care of? Some of us younger children of [the] Missouri Synod never realize what we have in our splendid supply of good and interesting books and periodicals, and many of us are as ungrateful as the nine lepers, because we do not read them as we should.

Under such conditions in Russia, so many of these German Russian children, children of God by their Baptism, grew up without really understanding the chief doctrines of their faith, without knowing why they were called Lutherans. True, there were many good Lutheran sermons read to them in their meetinghouses (which they call "schools," but which were not always used for school purposes), but they lacked the key to these sermons, hardly understanding their language, and thus got little or nothing out of them. And thus many of them had grown up within the visible

Lutheran Church, kept in it by custom and by a certain pressure exerted by the state, but heathens in their hearts, not believing that the Bible is God's Word and unwilling to be ruled by it. It is not easy for me to write this. It was not easy for me even to believe it. But my present purpose is not to whitewash but to tell the truth in painting the background of my work. I had set out to show why we speak of mission work among so-called Lutherans. And at the time of my arrival at Guarany [Guarani] a deplorable number of these thousand families had proved the truth of what I have written. Hundreds had gone over to the Baptist church, because they had easily been persuaded that their Lutheran faith was the faith which is without works and dead [cf. James 2:26]. Hundreds of others had felt the fetters of state control drop and had then thrown off the influence of good custom as equally oppressive and were now proving themselves to be real, 100 percent heathens.

And here I was, willing to become acquainted with this very interesting, if not always pleasant, sort of people. Before I had arrived, however, God had already built a special school for the purpose of helping me along in the first steps of my work. There was no parsonage ready for me, and I was offered the free use of a little vacant house for my first temporary abode. It belonged to an old water mill, and when I rode into the mill yard in a secluded valley, the miller—my teacher-to-be—stood in the doorway. Mertens was his name, and a very unusual man he was. I fear that, [despite] his friendly welcome, his first appearance did not give me the feeling of refreshment and keen pleasure that I now experience at the very thought of him. His figure was bent, and two almost fatal bodily accidents had doomed him to be called "Old Man" Mertens in the prime of his life by everybody [who] knows him. But I soon began to feel the refreshment that emanates from that great and wonderful soul. He had no school education. He was as blissfully innocent as most of his compatriots of all the laws and bylaws of grammar. But he reads, speaks, and writes four languages, not counting Yiddish, of which he is also a master. Large words sometimes fell crosswise on his tongue, or with one syllable crushed or inverted. But he got their sense all the better for not having to worry about their form. His memory is a miracle to me, and he seems never to have forgotten anything he ever saw, heard, or read. His reading would have filled a good five foot shelf and included half a dozen volumes of the St. Louis edition of Luther.[1] A ceaseless flow of spontaneous humor, genuine piety without Pietism, and a good repute with friend and foe were the crowning glories of this unique character.

Within his mill, he had what he himself calls a little mission post. With such a heart full of faith it couldn't be otherwise. He only improves a good opportunity. For to his mill come the representatives of all religious tendencies to have their corn

1 I.e., Johann Georg Walch, ed., *Dr. Martin Luthers sämmtliche Schriften: Neue revidirte Stereotypausgabe*, 23 vols. in 25 (Concordia Publishing House, 1880–1910).

ground. And while their grain fell between the millstones, usually the innermost thoughts of all these hearts were being ground between the stones of the miller's powerful mind. That came so naturally, and was such a thorough and painless process, that I, who love to take conversation into my own hands on other occasions, felt happy in sitting nearly spellbound on a sack of grain, sometimes for hours together, listening and enjoying and learning as I had never learned at the feet of my good professors. I learned to understand and to speak the particular brand of German that these people use. I became thoroughly acquainted with the good and bad sides of their characters. I learned to see the good kernel under the rough shell, whenever there was one. I became thoroughly conversant with the tricks and arguments used by the various enemies of true Lutheranism and had some powerful weapons against them put into my hands by that "old" miller-theologian. I underwent a thorough postgraduate course in the application of our Lutheran doctrine to the special new conditions that were confronting me in my work.

At first, I learned by listening only, but after a few months, I began to join in the conversation, doing the necessary practical exercises under the supervision of my teacher. On such occasions, after the mill customer had left, I would ask the miller-missionary whether my language had been clear and my arguments understood by those for whom they were intended. And he would always tell me, with absolute frankness, which of my words and phrases had been "too grammatical" for the hearer. My diploma I received about the end of my first year, when after a debate with a chief enemy that lasted from 7 a.m. to 7 p.m. without so much as an intermission to drink a glass of water, in which my teacher no longer saw fit to join in (and it was a proof of his wonderful tact that he didn't) but restricted himself to providing a few Lutheran witnesses—when after this debate he volunteered the statement that now I was being understood by my hearers. I felt more joy over this diploma than over the two Latin diplomas that I had received on other occasions.

Between the mill and the dwelling house there is an old kitchen, a small wooden shack with no floor, with battered doors and sashless, shuttered windows, one wall almost half consumed by fire. Before the remainder of this wall, a wire hung down from a rafter, at the lower end of which swung an old, black cast-iron kettle over an open fire, and around the fire lay our pack of dogs and cats, keeping guard over the kettle and basking in the warmth. They who are privileged to know the secret charms of this old kitchen still speak of it as "the witch's kitchen." But in that cauldron no beggar's gruel bubbled nor witch's charmed broth. Into it were put each morning our daily ration of Brazilian black beans and smoked bacon or spareribs. And every noon, just about when one's stomach would begin to make itself heard in unmistakable language, the ration would be deliciously ready to be transferred from the cauldron to the plates of the eaters. Oh, how that same hunger grips me here in beautiful New York, among this perplexing variety of things good to eat, at the very thought of those daily bean dinners and suppers, God's own gift to Brazil! And our way of eating was so easy and comfortable! Mr. Mertens was only a renter, his family living on his own "rural lot" at a small distance from the mill, so that we were a home without a mother. So we never ate at a table—all the more as we had none—but everybody came and filled his plate whenever he got ready. And everybody chose the posture he liked best, standing, sitting, or reclining in classical fashion. That reminds me of a picture I saw in that old witch's kitchen which might be worth a million if it were painted. We had a guest, a born Leipziger and [a] graduate from our seminary at Porto Alegre, Rev. Raschke. One day he had beat me to the flesh-and-bean pot. When I entered the kitchen, he sat there, a little humpbacked man on a low bench, with the precious bean plate on his knees. Right before him sat our dear little doggie Wackerlos, his well-trained, graceful nose in modest restraint immediately beneath the rim of the plate (a restraint that came all the more naturally as he lacked bodily length to reach higher). Back of him, and over him, our large, gaunt, only half-civilized cur Gaspodin Brasovitch, his barbaric snout held in the most unbecoming fashion right over the rim of the plate. Under Mr. Raschke's right arm our venerable, gray-haired Mother Puss had insinuated herself and was feasting on the scent of the beans. And under his left arm our mother kitty Narcissa, to the manor born, with at least three generations of culture in her blood, basked her shapely little nose in the perfume of the bacon. And Mr. Raschke was improving his time and mending his inner man, as Mr. Mertens would put it. There was one occasion in my life when I regretted not having a camera in running order, and this was the occasion.

The house by the old water mill was the starting point for my trips to the different mission posts, of which I had seventeen at first. For besides the thirteen in the crumb cake, there were four more at a distance of from eight to twenty saddle hours. These hours stand for about four miles each. In rainy weather, it takes much more than an hour to ride such an hour's distance. During my first year, I practically used up two horses, being on the road on the average five days in the week, mostly from morning to nearly midnight. After losing a third horse by an unintentional and unfortunate exchange, which left in my hands an ancient and bony plug that may have been a first cousin to Spark Plug of the funny papers [the newspaper comics section], I resolved to quit horses. I was lucky in getting two fine, large "Missouri" mules, imported from [the] Uruguay Republic. They were entirely unbroken and deathly afraid of any man except a [native Black trainer]. But the Brazilian horse tamers were also afraid of the mules, and I would not consent to have them tamed by being first starved half to death, which is a common practice. We hitched them up once to a wagonload of lumber in the company of other mules, and then the boys of Mr. Mertens rode them for the first time. After that they were taken into the service of the mission, although that meant taking my life into my own hand each time I saddled up and got on the half-tamed animals. But after they had gotten to know me, and I had developed a system of handling them, I had two beasts of burden that could not be killed, and I would not have exchanged them for the best half dozen of horses in Kentucky.

These trips on muleback were mostly interesting, which doesn't mean, however, that they were pleasant. Soon after the advent of the mules, I also moved into the parsonage, which was nearly half-finished at the time. From here I was called one day to baptize a little child at a place five miles away. There were no mudholes in the road, but rather the whole road was a single mudhole, knee-deep. This meant riding in a walk all the way. After the Baptism, the mother of the child desired to be communed. I had not brought any wine, and there was none to be had any nearer than the parsonage. There was nobody to send after wine—or, rather, there was no horse for anybody to ride. So there was nothing left but for me to ride back and get the necessary elements. When I again left that house after Communion, the sun was just setting. But there had been a marriage announced for the afternoon. To avoid any disappointment, I had left notice for the couple to proceed to the house of the bride's parents at once, on their way from the legal marriage, promising to come there as soon as I should be able. To save myself a mile of bad roads, I took a new bridle path, which was, however, in use long enough to have been converted into the same knee-deep mud. The night was dark. In that path, closed as it was on top by forest verdure, it was just as dark as in a tunnel of solid stone. Only by the splash-splash of the mule's feet could I tell at all that I was still in the road. I was very much on the alert, for I could but expect to have my skull bumped against some large branch, or one of my eyeballs against the protruding, sharpened end of some bamboo shoot. And I knew by experience that any unusual noise, such as the crackling of a broken reed, would make my young and [easily scared] mule begin a dash for dear life. The worst that happened for a long time was that my hat was knocked from my head by a bough, and I had to search for it in the dark. And thus I rode and rode and rode and still rode. Some things expand by heat, but miles expand by darkness. All at once my mule was standing on his hind feet and spinning around on them like a top. I couldn't do a thing to stop him. So I did the next best thing: I sat in the saddle and waited, knowing that it would not be possible for him to spin all night. And he didn't. When he stopped, I unraveled myself from the vines and got down. A tree had fallen across the path. I took for granted that there would already be an emergency bypath around the obstruction and tried to lead my mule to it. He refused to be led in the dark. I tied him to a sapling and found the bypath by tumbling into the mud and getting my boots filled. I was glad even at that. I returned to the mule and got into the saddle and rode over. But when I had gotten there, I knew absolutely nothing about the direction in which I had come. Nor about the direction that I was going. For a while I sat in the saddle and thought it over. No result. I thought it over real hard. No result yet. I thought it over still harder. Result. One ray of light in that fearful darkness: "Only one way can be wrong, so the other must be right." I rode off. And I rode and rode and rode and still rode. Then there came the first ray of physical light. I struck a wider road, open above. I had arrived. I recognized by a large log on the roadside that I was back at the place where I had seen the sun set. What could I do but take a good deep breath of relaxation and ride off by the longer way past the parsonage? In due time, shortly before midnight, I arrived at the bride's home, found the husband-to-be sound asleep in consequence of wearying drinks, and performed the marriage ceremony among interruptions by drunken guests.

On another occasion, I had bought a number of maps for my schools at Ijuhy [Ijuí]. To make sure that they would reach home in a dry state, I wrapped them up in my raincoat and sent them on with a driver. It was a fine, sunny day in winter. I intended to take a roundabout way, raising the distance to twenty hours. But I meant to ride this distance without a stop, keeping at it all night, in order not to miss the hour of catechism instruction at home. Toward evening it began to drizzle, and the darker it got, the harder it rained, and the harder it rained, the colder it got. And poor me with only a khaki riding suit! At about seven o'clock we, meaning the mule [and I], fell into a ditch. I have always maintained that this was intentional on the part of the mule. But I did not want to risk it again. By the momentary illumination of a streak of lightning, I picked out a thornbush under which to seek shelter. Not that it was raining less fiercely there, but still there is a certain feeling of protection under a bush, in the midst of the wide plain, in rain and lightning and thunder. In order not to tire, I stood first on my eastern leg and then changed about to the western one. The mule did about the same. After nearly twelve hours of this changing about the morning dawned, and the rain abated and finally stopped. The warm sun went to work on my wet clothes, and when, after ten more hours in the saddle, I reached home, I had no need to fear a scolding for having gotten my nice clothes wet. I even found a long rod of iron on the road, picked it up, and returned it to the driver who had lost it, making him very happy.

Thirteen preaching posts in my immediate surroundings were just about eight too many. That they existed (besides a number of [union] church schools) was due to the fact that the people had been ruled with an iron hand from above when still in Russia and therefore knew as little about the practical administration of congregations as they mostly did about doctrine. Besides there was the lack of crossroads in the new settlement. The walls of unbroken forest split into three long and narrow congregations what should have been a single one of a nearly square shape. I soon realized that by preaching at so many places I was only frittering away my physical and mental powers. As a rule, I could only get a hearing once in four to six months, counting in the rainy Sundays, which wasn't much better than the pastors in Russia had been doing. And between my visits few and far between, the good seed of the Word would easily have been snowed under by the tares of some false prophet, who had his opportunity once or twice every week.

In the old "witch's kitchen," we were soon busily deliberating on the ways and means of a more practical organization of the entire Lutheran Church within the crumb cake of Guarany [Guarani]. The founding of one large central congregation with its headquarters at or near the parsonage that was being built by [the Missouri]

Synod, and the gradual addition of as many more smaller congregations round about, probably about four, seemed to be the natural thing to aim at. The only practical step I could take while living at the old mill was to call together the presidents of the thirteen so-called congregations in order to gain their consent and enlist their interest in the plan. While this may not have been entirely in vain, I cannot say that it brought much progress.

The moment I had taken my residence in the half-finished parsonage, I was in a position to go ahead with other measures. The first was to organize what we called a night school. The more progressive younger men of the different "congregations" were invited to meet every Friday night in the pastor's study. We studied German reading, spelling, and grammar and some Portuguese. We had a few minutes of parliamentary drill, so as to get ourselves accustomed to chairmen, secretaries, roll calls, motions, putting the question, and the like, which were quite new ideas to most of the members. I also began the serial reading of some of the stories of Alfred Ira, treating some of the problems of congregational life in such masterly fashion. To ensure the attendance and attentiveness of all members as far as possible, we drank our Brazilian tea during these readings.

This tea consists of the powdered leaves and twigs of the the South American [yerba] maté or Paraguay tea.[2] This tea, which makes a splendid substitute for oriental tea when drunk as a weak decoction, is usually taken in South America in a much stronger form. A small gourd or other suitable vessel is filled with the tea powder, just leaving room on one side to insert a silver tube with a sort of a sieve at the lower end. Then the remaining air space is filled with nearly boiling water. The resulting strong decoction is then sucked from the tube. The host takes the first filling, then refills the gourd in turn for every guest. The drink tastes rather bitter to the newcomer, and the manner of so many different people sucking from the same tube may seem to the average North American like a veiled way of committing suicide. But in many parts of South America this is a sacred rite of hospitality, and once you have become accustomed to the taste and captivated by the habit and the stimulant power of the beverage, I know of no other drink in the world that brings with it the same measure of democratic sociability as this. I am not advocating its introduction into the civilized world, as I think it contains too much tannic acid (11 percent) to be wholesome. But we introduced it with a purpose in our meetings, and I am sure it helped to make them a success. The main purpose of the school was to become acquainted with one another and to get an opportunity to talk over the plan of organization. In

2 Pastor Lehenbauer is referring here to chimarrão, a traditional drink from southern Brazil and other South American countries. It is prepared by infusing ground yerba mate, served with hot water in a gourd, and consumed through a metal straw called a bomba. This beverage holds great cultural significance, with its preparation and consumption ritual symbolizing tradition and companionship.

this we succeeded. Not only are some of the former night scholars at present the most active and understanding members of our rebuilt congregations, but some of them are doing service as chairmen and secretaries.

Next we solved the mail problem and began our circulating library. Even after the completion of the new stretch of railroad ("My Railroad"), the parsonage was [an eleven-hour] ride from the nearest station, four hours from the nearest government post office, and three hours from the nearest telephone. Frequently my mail made a long and dangerous roundabout trip before it found me. And if there is one thing in the world that gets on my nerves it is a poor postal service. So it was but natural for me to work out a plan for a model private postal system, which was to bring us our mail directly from the post office once a week. After various experiences, one of which I described in the *Atlantic Monthly* at the time,[3] the mail became, as it should be, something sacred and charming, and for years it has been arriving at the parsonage every Friday evening, rain or shine, to be distributed to all the congregations on Saturday or Sunday morning. At first, the night school men did the distributing; later on, the teachers. And now we had an organization by which we could successfully hope to introduce good periodicals and books into the homes and, later on, carry on various activities serving a dignified publicity for our church and school work. [Despite] hindering war measures, we succeeded in getting a fair number of periodicals introduced. And the books of the circulating library were nearly always "out." I know of a number of young people who, not having had the opportunity to go to school in their childhood, now learned to read so well by means of this library that they were not afraid to tackle very thick books. And parents who could not read themselves could now enjoy wonderful literature by hearing it read by their children.

But as the need of real schools was the greatest need of all, the teachers' conference was the keystone of all our organization work. A small number of so-called teachers had been brought along from Russia, and they were kept in office and respected as an heirloom by the congregations as long as possible. Mostly they knew nothing at all of good teaching methods, their chief teachers' and pupils' help being the stick. In the course of years, the supply of this valuable class of humanity ran out. We deplored the fact that [the] Synod had no teachers for us to fill the vacancies as they appeared. But we did not lose much time in deploring. A number of younger men who could read and even write were chosen. Most of them did not have school education in their boyhood days. But they were willing to make up for lost time as far as possible. And I was more than willing to give them the chance. We gathered in conference at the parsonage every Saturday. There we began at the beginning, going through the things a child must learn the very first weeks and months of its school life. This was necessary not only in order to show the men how to impart this knowledge to the children

3 See Albert Lehenbauer, letter to the editor, *Atlantic Monthly* (June 1917), 3.

but also because I had discovered that they needed it for their own sakes. Thus we were startled one fine day by finding that one of our older men, having taught school for several years, did not know that every sentence must begin with a capital letter. After that discovery, I should not have been surprised at all to find him spelling his own name "wlAdislaW steinbRennEr." This was not the only discovery made. But we soon showed progress. Schoolwork began to move in a healthy pulsation, where before it had gone by fits and starts. Parents began to prick up their ears. Chance visitors to the schools noticed that the teacher never sat in his easy chair (meaning the hard wooden bench behind his desk) but was on his feet every minute of the school day. It surprised them that he seldom or never used the stick, except for pointing. It surprised them still more that children were learning more [despite] this oversight than they had ever dreamed possible before. They were delighted when their boys and girls brought home wonderful storybooks and read them to their parents almost as fluently and intelligibly as the teacher or pastor himself. But the limit was reached when they attended the public examinations and saw their own little tots, among other things, spell the most difficult words in the German language without books [and] in the most cocksure manner possible. Who had ever experienced that even in a dream in Russia? And even Portuguese words. And they read and translated Portuguese without a hitch. Why, the old staple argument of the wise old men began to lose its pull: "I can't read nor write, and I've come all the way from Russia to Brazil. I don't see why my children should know more than I." A healthy jealousy sprang up between parents: the neighbor's children must not be able to read better than one's own; and therefore one's own must not be suffered to attend less regularly than the neighbor's. It became necessary to remind parents that they must not send their children too young. Last year, six families in one congregation were sending thirty children to school. The whole congregation of twenty-eight members was sending seventy-two children. And it was a mighty rainy day indeed when the attendance was not actually above sixty. Sometimes on a rainy day the teacher would stay at the house, thinking that he might expect a day of rest. But he would be fooled, for the children would come and get him from the house. Parents complained to the pastor that they could not keep their children at home when they needed them. I suppose I need not say that there were some parents, and a few children, that did not join in with this general wave of school enthusiasm.

And then came our choirs. God sent a man to the parsonage, a worthless creature otherwise, but music-loving and music-trained and endowed with a voice by the grace of God. For several years he curbed his bad inclinations—alcoholism among them—to such an extent as to permit him to conduct and inspire our choirs, until in later years the pastor's time permitted him to take over this work. In the course of about six years, our seven different choirs sang hundreds of the world's choicest compositions, the chorales of Bach's *Passion according to St. Matthew* among others. The singers were always filled with enthusiasm and hardly realized what difficult and splendid work they were doing. We never lost sight of the chief goal we had set for ourselves, to further the organization of the congregations by means of the choirs. We did that in leading the people to our services, in training the congregations in singing our splendid old Lutheran chorales in the original manner, and in utilizing the rehearsals for fruitful discussions [of] congregational problems. As an important side issue, we succeeded in crowding the Moody-and-Sankey-style hymns out of favor, which had been brought over in abominable German translations and were beloved for their ear-tickling melodies and their leg-inspiring rhythms.[4]

Not without conflict did we gain these results. I shall have space to mention only the most important, and them very briefly. There was the fight against local patriotism. Everybody was willing to unite into larger congregations, to be sure. But everybody wanted everybody else to come the whole way. "It must be on our street, in our school!" It was against this enemy that our singing proved to be a strong weapon.

Then there was the fight against the Pietists and self-appointed preachers, especially the so-called "Brethren" (*Gemeinschaftsbrüder*), who were so holy in their own sight as to be in danger of flying to heaven in their working clothes. They were tugging away at Christ's net with all their might, but unfortunately in the wrong direction. Most of them became Baptists and, later on, freethinkers.

There were fights all along the line with those who were sooner or later revealed as frank unbelievers. These were in the majority in many of the smaller "congregations," and in some cases the Lutheran minority lost their church property. In others, the property had to be sold and the proceeds divided up. In such cases, it was the rule to blame the pastor for having caused the dissensions. In all cases, this blame rests easy on his back. It was the Word of God that they were fighting against, and God it was [who] gave the victory to His Word in all cases, though not always in the same manner. His power was at all times too plainly to be felt for the pastor or any of the members to lay claim to any credit. And He not only caused the storms to break and the sunshine to return at the right times, but He also made His true Lutherans, a number small but not to be despised, to see that there was no other way to peace than through the fight.

That the pastor's personal life was not always a path strewn with roses the reader will not have to be told. But I want to mention a few details, not in order to put my person on the pedestal but in order to justify the title "Roughing It." It will not be going wrong to mention the mental side of "roughing it" in the first place. I fear the reader can hardly imagine what it means for a man, whose mind and soul has been developed into an appreciation of all that is good and noble and full of

4 For more on these popular gospel hymns of the late nineteenth century (some from the evangelist Dwight L. Moody and the song leader Ira D. Sankey), see James L. Brauer, "America to 1960," in *Lutheran Service Book: Companion to the Hymns* (Concordia Publishing House, 2019), 2:74.

intellectual content, developed by what to him will always seem an exceptional home, by a good teacher and pastor, by nearly a score of professors who were mostly excellent men, developed unto all good things for more than twenty years—I say, you can hardly imagine what it means to such a person to be suddenly dumped in the wilds of southern Brazil, among people whose outstanding qualities are illiteracy, drunkenness, superficiality, and the coarsest coarseness of language and manners. Before I got my call to Brazil, I spent nearly a year among the hoboes, fruit tramps, and other roughnecks of our own Wild West. The reader will pardon me if I don't explain here how I got into such company. I know now what I didn't know then, that it was another of God's own schools for my work in Brazil. But I just want to say that these hoboes cannot hold the candle to some of my German Russians in the coarseness of their language. I have sometimes felt thankful that it was not my luck to have to take an American girl into this atmosphere, though that is not saying that a true-blue American girl, if she were placed into such an atmosphere by the will of God, could not after all be perfectly happy in His service there. And lest I forget the bright side, I want to remind myself and the reader that this dreary waste of illiteracy and coarseness had a pleasant oasis for me in the person of Mr. Mertens, who was really my only "company" during my first year or two.

I have already given a few samples of what the many cruel rides meant, to which the missionary is subjected in his work. I should like to recur to the subject once more in all seriousness, without taking any of the edge off the roughness, by showing a humorous side. I have never felt these long and cruel rides so much as a sacrifice on my part as I felt them to [be] an unconscionable waste of forces that belong to God. The missionary's powers for the efficient fulfillment of his manifold duties, his bodily powers, his nerve force, his mental freshness are all so inexcusably curtailed by his being bumped up and down in the saddle hour after hour. Once, in a weak hour during one of these rides, I counted the steps of my mule in one minute and multiplied this number by the number of minutes in ten hours, a ride that I had to make so often: a total of some ninety thousand bumps. It would be folly to believe that a human being could preach as powerfully or instruct as well or be as wide-awake to his opportunities for doing pastoral work on individuals after so many bumps up and down as he would if the shocks of the road had, for the greater part, been taken up by a set of good buggy springs. That's what it comes down to finally: so much of the missionaries' powers wasted, scattered on the road, for the lack of a set of buggy springs under him. And we can't buy buggies in Brazil, and the individual missionary cannot import them, and the mission board has no money to send them, or something else is wrong somewhere. The missionary doesn't know where the hitch really is. But it makes his heart sick, not that his dear old carcass is suffering but that the Lord's work is not being done as it should be.

If I may be pardoned for writing a few more words on a somewhat painful subject, I should like to call attention to the cruelest part of such a cruel ride. It is the coming home in the pitchy darkness, in pouring rain, on roads where every step may bring death. I don't mean death by wild animals. I have never met a dangerous animal nor been attacked by robbers. I mean the dangers of breaking your skull or neck on an overhanging limb, the danger of cutting your throat on a split reed, the danger of slipping, falling, being dragged to death by the animal you are riding. I am not indulging in fancies. I have been miraculously saved from all these and other dangers too many times. I am not making a bid for sympathy. I have been so happy in my work each day of those eight years that I wouldn't know what to do with sympathy if I had it. I only want to say what I started out to say, that these rides in the dark, for hours together, with the dangerous uncertainty hanging over your head are the most cruel part of our cruel life in the saddle, and one hour of this always seemed to tear down my nerve more than five hours by daylight or without rain or on good, level roads. And then I want to point out that in most cases, where the road is wide enough for a wagon at all, a buggy with a lamp attached would do away with most of this strain on the nerves.

My home life too contained enough of the rough stuff to keep it from becoming flat and insipid. In a former paragraph, I referred to our way of living in the old mill. Later on, at the parsonage, I had more of the feeling of [my] own home, but I had to get along for a few years with male servants of various kinds, who also did the cooking in various ways. One of them had a craze for soups, made excellent cottage cheese, firmly believed that my cow was bewitched, and had a habit of drying his socks on the coffee can. Later on I had a cook that knew how to cook, but he had other faults, as, for instance, helping himself to the contents of my money drawer, which was no great harm, as a missionary's money drawer is nearly always empty.

The parsonage was well meant by [the] Synod's representatives: a large, two-story building of sixteen rooms, intended to house two missionaries, with the greatest number of large French windows that I ever saw in a house of that size. With the exception of my study, the windows were without glass during the war and for some time after. There were no shutters. In Brazil, it rains at times. We sometimes have the feeling as if it were always raining there, and with every rain the water would pour down through the ceiling on the windward side of the house. In some rains, all four sides seemed windward, as the storm drove the sheets of rain through from end to end. But we were trained, like a ship's crew, to stow all movable goods away on the driest side of the house. And when the wind changed, we would re-stow them on the other side. And sometimes we would be sitting on the leeward side and wouldn't notice the rain coming in on the windward, and would then find some books ruined or a bed wet through and through or even covered with a layer of clay mortar from the unfinished wall. That, too, was hard on the nerves. But I can say that I always tried to find a funny side. One of the funny sides was this, that the floor was absolutely waterproof. We had to bore holes through it to get the water out. But after I had a wife, and before I got the idea of the holes in the floor, and whenever we would have stowed the goods away on a dry side, before the wind would have had a chance to turn, we would join hands and dance around barefoot in the sea on the floors of study and dining room. That was a funny side; but I sometimes had my doubts whether most women would have thought it funny. But after all, I had a home, and it was always a real home to me. And after eight years of building, the house is now nearly finished, and it rains into the rooms very seldom now, and into the beds hardly at all anymore.

I have already broken the news that after some years of bachelor's life I found a mother for the home. In those four lonesome years, I sometimes worried how any woman at all would find me in the Brazilian backwoods in order to get married to me. These worries, like all worries, were unnecessary altogether. Just at the right time God provided, without any aid on my part, that the dearest girl in all the wide, wide world (for me) became the neighboress of my parsonage. Quite naturally the inevitable was not slow in happening then. When we were engaged, a number of deputations from congregation members appeared, demanding that the engagement be broken again, as they did not intend to accept a girl from the congregation as wife of their pastor. And there came deputations of nonmembers, demanding that we keep the engagement, as they would involve us in newspaper scandal if we didn't. Both kinds of deputations didn't alter the course of history in the least.

We both had no money for a so-called wedding. On the evening of our legal marriage, we entertained only each other. Five days later we rode together to Ijuhy [Ijuí], where we were married in church on what we call our official wedding day. And a simple but unforgettably beautiful wedding was prepared for us by Rev. Müller and his wife, and teacher Naumann and his wife. Among the guests were several pastors and teachers on their way to a conference. We were persuaded to travel along to the conference. On our return, we borrowed Rev. Müller's buggy for the last one hundred miles. Being in Brazil, it was not surprising that we should have our front axle bent when crossing the first river. The next thing was that my mules walked out into the center of a large pond, then stood and looked at me as if to say, "Come and get us if you want us," which I did. Next, we got stuck in stiff mud up to the axles at one of the rivers, the mules pulled like sixty, and both singletrees broke like toothpicks. I think that this was done intentionally on the part of the mules. At all events, we were forced to get down into the mud over our knees and lift the wagon out. And next, one of those real Brazilian rains began to pour down, which continued until we arrived at home. That was our honeymoon trip. We have been living very happy ever afterward.

If I had the space, I should like to write a thing or two about that wonderful woman who is my wife. But the most important things are to be found recorded in the last chapter of the book of Proverbs. May, I add, that she is a German Russian by birth, a Brazilian by adoption since her eleventh year, an American by sympathies and by marriage. Having had no school, she is a wonderful reader. In her confirmation days and after she memorized all of the synodical catechism, including most of Luther's introduction. In her girlhood days, she made fourteen miles afoot and back on the same day—in the rain and barefoot, of course—to hear one of our [choir] concerts. As a mother, she is one of the most up-to-date scientific child raisers I know of. I know I shall be pardoned for divulging so much of the family history, because I have been asked by good and interested women: "Have you a good wife?"

We have been asked other questions, one or two of which I shall answer here. "Don't you wear wedding rings in Brazil?" Yes, we do. At least those people do [who] have the money. We didn't have it at the time. Later on we made up our minds that we would have sweet revenge for this condition of affairs by buying our rings at no other place than Tiffany's in New York. Which we did. They are the usual gold bands and contain the legend: "Urwahnfried—1918." Nothing else, but that is a volume. *Urwahnfried* is a word composed of old German word roots and means in modern English "fulfillment," or, more explicitly, "the place where my fight for the highest and broadest ideals of life came to an end in the peace of victory." *Urwahnfried* is the name of the parsonage at Guarany [Guarani]. It is also the name of our private postal station, which is very important, as formerly much of our mail went to a little town on the border of [the] Uruguay Republic by the name of Quarahy [Quaraí]. Since the adoption of our own name, I know of no case of mail going astray in this manner.

We have been asked whether there are physicians and midwives and nurses in Brazil. I think little Siegfried calls forth these questions, the little sunny child of the forest with the dancing eyes, who knows not how extremely unfortunate he is in having been born in the forest primeval without either a doctor or a nurse. Our nearest doctor was sixty miles away, which means thirty to sixty hours back and forth, according to the weather. We must give this man credit for having caused us neither trouble nor worry in all those years. For when we needed him, we could not get to him. And when we could get to him, we didn't need him. And to have him come to us would have cost about a month's salary. Of midwives there were all too many within the crumb cake of Guarany [Guarani], but only one among them with any training or reading at all. Some of the rest brought with them the full night of medieval ignorance and superstition. Just to mention one case that will suffice to give Americans the shudders: one of the busiest of them all would lay the newborn babes out on the cold floor practically without wraps for about an hour in order to give the evil spirits an opportunity to evaporate. We preferred, for reasons that seem valid to us, to welcome little Siegfried by ourselves. In all essential things he received the same reception that he would have enjoyed at a good hospital, and God did the rest. We should be guilty of dishonesty to say that we had wished it to be otherwise.

As for my own health, I had contracted a hemorrhage of the stomach as early as 1916, a consequence of those long, cruel horseback rides. In passing, I may mention that in the time of greatest weakness, being in danger of fainting every second, I was forced to stand up and perform a marriage ceremony. [Despite] this and other things I became well. But in 1922 I had four relapses, usually at a distance of from eight to ten hours from home and [with] no way of getting there but on horseback (at least no better way). Every attack took me to death's door and kept me in a condition of extreme weakness for a month or more. When I received permission to take a year's furlough, I had had one attack, and when the money arrived after eight or nine months, the other three were over. I went to a good hospital in Germany, and after a week's thorough examination, I was agreeably surprised to hear that there was absolutely no trace of any defect in my stomach. As there could be no doubt at all of the reality of the hemorrhages, the hospital physicians seemed unable to rhyme the case with their theories. To me this rhyming is easy, for I believe in miracles. The doctors would have enjoyed ever so much to perform an operation on me as a reserve for a possible next appearance, which I politely declined.

In conclusion of this short history of eight years of roughing it for Christ in the wilds of Brazil, I feel that I should not omit a word of Christ that every missionary knows and believes and values. It is recorded [in] Mark 10:29–30: "Verily I say unto you, There is no man that hath left house, or brethren, or sisters, or father, or mother, or wife, or children, or lands, for My sake, and the gospel's, but he shall receive an hundredfold now in this time, houses, and brethren, and sisters, and mothers, and children, and lands, with persecutions; and in the world to come eternal life." I cannot say how much I am refreshed by a return into the full enjoyment of the manifold blessings of civilization during my stay in Germany and the United States, nor how grateful I am for all the kindness shown me by the brothers on both sides of the Atlantic. But there is no place just like *Urwahnfried*, and there is no substitute for the special blessing of God in the mission field. My heart's desire and my daily prayer is to be back at work soon after these pages shall have appeared in print, there where I have already chosen my burial place. The only thing that is more satisfying and blessed than roughing it for Christ is—*more* roughing it for Christ.

Albert Ernst Heinrich Lehenbauer

Abrindo Fronteiras para Cristo nas Selvas do Brasil

[Jesus disse:] "Vocês serão minhas testemunhas . . . até os confins da terra."
(Atos 1:8)

Traduzido por
CLAUDIO FLOR

Editado por
RAPHAEL VOIGT

A Série de Monografias do Instituto Histórico Concordia existe para publicar e disseminar pesquisas significativas e cativantes relacionadas à história da Igreja Luterana Confessional na América do Norte, especialmente aquelas que utilizam o material preservado pelo arquivo e biblioteca do Instituto Histórico Concordia, assim como materiais mantidos pelos arquivos e bibliotecas de outras entidades da Igreja Luterana—Sínodo de Missouri.

Daniel N. Harmelink, Editor da Série

John C. Wohlrabe Jr., Lawrence R. Rast Jr, John W. Sias, Editores Associados

OUTROS VOLUMES DA SÉRIE

Seminex in Print: A Comprehensive Bibliography of Published Material and Selected Archival Resources for Historical Research. Compiled by David O. Berger with Daniel N. Harmelink (2021).

The Emigration of the Saxon Lutherans in the Year 1838 and Their Settlement in Perry County, Missouri by J. F. Koestering. Translated by Brian Lutz and G. H. Naumann. Revised for publication by Matthew Carver (2022).

Rediscovering the Issues Surrounding the 1974 Concordia Seminary Walkout. Edited by Ken Schurb (2023).

A Hundredfold Harvest: A Survey of Mission Work in Travancore, South India, in the Early 1900s. Heinrich Nau. Translated by Matthew Carver (2025).

Publicado originalmente como *Roughing It for Christ in the Wilds of Brazil*, Zwickau: Johannes Herrmann, 1923.

As citações bíblicas são da versão Nova Almeida Atualizada, publicada pela Sociedade Bíblica do Brasil.

Todas as fotografias deste livro aparecem com a permissão da família Lehenbauer.

Produzido nos Estados Unidos da América.

Albert Ernst Heinrich Lehenbauer

(13 de fevereiro de 1891—29 de abril de 1955)

ALBERT ERNST HEINRICH LEHENBAUER nasceu em West Ely, no estado de Missouri, nos Estados Unidos da America, no dia 13 de Fevereiro de 1891, e foi um dos oito filhos de Conrad e Catherine (Preusser) Lehenbauer. Aos 5 anos de idade, seu pai faleceu e dai por diante sua mãe providenciou, que depois de sua confirmação no Domingo de Ramos, em 1905, pelo pastor Pflanz, ele iniciasse sua educação pre-teológica em Concordia, no estado de Missouri. Ali ele estudou por 5 anos antes de ingressar no seminário em Saint Louis (também em Missouri) e se formar em teologia em 1913. Desejava muito aceitar um chamado para o exterior. Na verdade queria ser missionário na China. Porém, antes de deixar o país em direção ao Oriente, decidiu ficar mais um ano na sua Terra Natal. Neste meio tempo a situação política mundial deteriou (como o prezado leitor dever estar lembrado, a Primeira Guerra Mundial iniciou em 1914) e não foi mais possível enviar missionarios para China. Isto fez com que o pastor Albert decidisse aceitar um chamado para o Brasil, onde seus dois irmãos, Conrad (que foi pastor em Arroio do Meio) e George (que foi pastor em Santa Cruz), ja serviam no campo de missão antes da sua chegada. O leitor deve estar lembrado também de haver lido neste livrinho, que meu avô chegou em Porto Alegre no dia 2 de Fevereiro de 1915, Dia de Nossa Senhora dos Navegantes, um feriado. Como não falava português e o comércio estava fechado, teve grande dificuldade em localizar o nosso seminário. Depois de visitar seus dois irmãos por curto tempo, o pastor Albert viajou de trem para Ijuí, onde o pastor E. Müller estava aguardando a sua chegada. De la foi de charrete para Linha 23, e Guarany, onde sua primeira pregação em Abril daquele mesmo ano foi baseada no Evangelho de São Lucas 18:9-14, uma passagem que tão claramente descreve o amor e a graça de Deus. Sobre este mesmo amor e graça de Deus o pastor Albert Lehenbauer pregou, ensinou e escreveu durante todos seus anos de ministério, sendo um grande exemplo para seus congregandos em Linha 15, ou seja, Urwahnfried, como ele chamava o lugar, e também para os seus 13 outros pontos de missão. E foi também esta a razão porque iniciou reuniões com homens jovens, que prometiam ser aptos a entrar no pastorado, ensinado-os as doutrinas cristãs nas noites de Domingo sempre que possível.

Por acreditar na importância da boa leitura na formação cristã, o pastor Albert foi o primeiro editor do "Luther-Kalender." Ele também escreveu um grande número de artigos para o "Kirchenblatt," "Leitor Brasileiro," e tanto quanto seu tempo lhe permitia fazer, ele escreveu muitos outros artigos que foram publicados em jornais da igreja dentro e fora do Brasil. Sua clara e simples maneira de escrever refletia sua fé na doutrina Biblica e nos ensinamentos de Martinho Lutero.

Devido as seus muitos e variados dons, logo foi eleito membro do comitê de missão, e pouco tempo depois foi eleito diretor do departamento de missão no Brasil. Além disto serviu no cargo de vice-presidente da igreja no Brasil de 1928 a 1932. Devido a estes cargos, ele teve a oportunidade de viajar muito não só no Rio Grade do Sul mas também no exterior.

No dia 31 de Dezembro de 1918 o pastor Albert se casou com Helene Priebe. Seis dos seus oito filhos nasceram no Brasil (Urwahnfried). Seu segundo filho, Reginald, nasceu em Hannibal, Missouri (1923), enquanto meu avô estava de licensa nos Estados Unidos. Seu filho mais moço, Winfred, nasceu depois que ele havia aceito um chamado para Argentina (1939).

Foi quando voltou ao Brasil do seu ano de licensa, em 12 de novembro de 1923, com sua esposa Helene e seus dois filhos, Siegfried e Reginald, que o pastor Albert trouxe consigo uma garrafa contendo grãos de soja. Ele havia notado que em alguns lugares, onde os seus membros haviam plantado varios diferentes tipos de grãos por alguns anos, que a terra estava exaurida e por este motivo produzia pouco ou quase nada. Assim se esmerou em pequisar uma solução para este problema. Como tinha o hábito de ler muito, descobriu que certas plantas adicionam nitrogênio ao solo, e portanto, suas raízes produzem adubo para terras exauridas, crescendo inclusive onde nada mais cresce. Descobriu que uma das plantas que se beneficiam da terra desta maneira é a soja. Foi assim, que o pastor Lehenbauer teve a idéia que o plantio da soja seria uma boa solução para seus membros revitalizarem as sùas terras exauridas. Ao chegar de volta em Urwahnfried, ele logo plantou as sementes que havia trazido. Em 1924, ao colher suas primeiras sementes plantadas em sua horta, o pastor ficou com a metade delas para plantar novamente, e distribuiu em caixinhas de fósforo dois our tres grãos de soja a varios dos seus congregandos. Para cada um que recebia as sementinhas ele dizia que eles deveriam plantá-las, e quando produzissem, ele queria que dividissem metade das sementes com seus vizinhos e amigos, e que eles por sua vez, fizessem o mesmo assim que inciassem a colher o grão na próxima safra.

A soja, em pouco tempo se multiplicou muito, tanto assim que havia fazendeiros que diziam colher, em alguns casos, de um so pé de soja, mais que 400 vagens. Não sabendo exatamente o que fazer com esta grande abundância de grãos, alguns dos seus congregandos tentaram fazer uma espécie de "café," primeiro torrando as sementes e então tentando moê-las. Infelizmente as pedras dos seus moinhos ficavam cobertas de uma pasta oleosa e apesar de todo seu esforço, desta forma produziam apenas uma quantidade mínima de pó ou farinha de soja. Mas muito pior era o fato de que quando usavam este farelo de soja para fazer "café," este se tornava absolutamente intragável, pois continha uma grossa e inapetitosa camada de óleo. Outros tentaram usar este tipo de pasta ou farinha de soja para fazer pão. Isto até que funcionou. Isto é, funcionou por um dia ou dois, mas quando o pão tinha mais que dois dias (pão velho, como se diz), se tornava tão oleoso que não dava gosto de ser ser comido, e só servia para ser jogado fora. Finalmente, não sabendo o que fazer com o grão de soja e não querendo perguntar ao seu pastor (uma coisa bem típica dos alemães daquela época, que tinham tanto respeito por seu pastor, que jamais pensariam sequer em questionar o que ele les dizia), alguém decidiu dar a semente de soja de comida a seus porcos. Isto, em pouco tempo causou uma verdadeira revolução na indústria suína do estado, pois os porcos não só cresceram, mas também engordaram em tempo recorde. O mesmo aconteceu com a indústria de gado leiteiro e de corte. Eventualmente a soja comecou a ser usada para farer-se azeite de cozinha, ao passo que o farelo que sobrava da extração de óleo, passou então a ser o produto principal que se dava aos suínos e equinos (farelo de soja). Dai por diante não houve mais como parar o plantio da soja no Brasil.

Hoje, o Brasil, é o segundo maior produtor mundial de soja, e a Argentina esta colocada em terceiro lugar. Sem dúvida, este grão mudou a vida dos colonos de Urwahnfried, e não só no Rio Grande do Sul, mas também em varios outros estados do Brasil, bem como na Argentina e até no Paraguay. Hoje a soja continua a trazer grandes divizas ao Brasil, e é usada na produção de um grande número de produtos alimentícios, bem como em uma grande e muito variada quantidade de outros produtos que pouco ou nada tem a ver com a alimentação.

Depois de ser pastor no Brasil por 22 anos, no início de1937, o pastor Albert Lehenbauer aceitou um chamado para ser diretor de uma escola pre teologica na Argentina (Colégio Concordia). Na época, a Argentina não tinha um seminário próprio. Isto queria dizer que todos pastores na Argentina eram formados no Brasil ou procediam dos Estados Unidos. Porém, a igreja estava muito interessada em chamar alguém que pudesse ajudar na educação preparatória e eventual formação de pastores de língua hispânica. A idéia era formar pastores que soubessem falar castelhano para suprir a igreja Argentina, e eventualmente também as outras nações da América Latina, cuja língua oficial é o espanhol. Esta escola foi iniciada em Villa Crespo, e o pastor Albert foi seu presidente de 1937 a 1942. Em 1942, quando viajou para os Estados Unidos, o pastor Lehenbauer finalmente conseguiu convencer o departamento de missão da igreja mãe da grande necessidade de se construir um seminário na Argentina. Quando finalmente o Seminário Concordia foi construido na Villa Ballester, nos arredores de Buenos Aires, inclusive com dependências para alguns professores, o pastor Albert foi o seu primeiro diretor. Ele exerceu este cargo de 1942 até 1946. Depois de 1946 ele foi professor de teologia do seminário até que faleceu.

Durante seus anos de pastorado na Argentina, o pastor Albert também foi co-editor do "Kirchengebote" (1938–1940), editor do Hinário Ev. Luterano, sendo que incluiu neste hinario alguns dos hinos que pessoalmente havia traduzido para o espanhol. Ele também encontrou tempo para ser co-editor de varios livros editados tanto em português como em espanhol durante este período, e escreveu varios artigos que foram lidos em conveções das igrejas tanto no Brasil como na Argentina.

Durante a convenção do jubileu da igreja Argentina em 1955 (50 anos da fundação da igreja Argentina), realizada na Aldea San Juan, em Entre Rios, o pastor Lehenbauer estava encarregado de fazer a devoção de encerramento. Esta foi a sua última função oficial na igreja, pois pouco antes de embarcar no trem de volta para Buenos Aires, ele sentiu fortes dores de cabeça, como nunca havia sentido antes na vida. Seus dois irmãos, George e Conrad, e também os seus dois genros, o pastor Fernando Höhn e o pastor Edgar Kroger, estavam com ele. Apesar de que seus genros quizessem levá-lo ao hospital, ele achou melhor seguir direto para Buenos Aires, pensando que tudo passaria em pouco tempo. Como suas dores de cabeça pioraram durante a viagem de trem, seus genros tentaram amomodá-lo no vagão de bagagens, onde seria mais confortavel para o pastor Lehenbauer ficar deitado. Chovia torrencialmente. Quando se deu conta que a sua situação estava piorando, o pastor Albert pediu sua Bíblia e leu as palavras do Salmo 23, bem como também o versiculo do Salmo 119:105. Pouco depois disto a sua língua não o obedecia mais, e dai por diante não teve mais condição de falar. O pastor R. Hasse perguntou ao pastor Albert se ele tinha fé em Jesus Cristo. Não podendo mais responder com palavras, o pastor Albert não hesitou em fazer um sinal positivo com sua cabeça. Apesar de tentar comunicar-se mais vezes, ninguém podia mais entendê-lo. Em pouco tempo se tornou inconsciente, e veio a falecer no hospital em Buenos Aires tres dias depois (40 horas mais tarde) devido a um derrame. O pastor Albert Lehenbauer faleceu no dia 29 de Abril de 1955. O seu funeral foi realizado no seminário, em Jose Leon Suarez, em San Martin, na Argentina. Três pregações diferentes foram feitas na ocasião. O presidente Rev. F. Lange pregou em espanhol, o Rev. S. H. Beckmann pregou em alemão e o Rev. Dr. R. Hasse pregou em português, ao passo que Rev. Enr. Hoapp oficiou o culto fúnebre e o enterro. O pastor Albert Lehenbauer foi sepultado no cemitério da cidade, em San Martin, na Argentina.

Planejando o que queria fazer no futuro, após se aposentar, meu avô havia comprado um pedaço de terra e construido uma casinha em Missiones. Enquanto minha avó Helena queria criar patos, galinhas e vacas, meu avô queria se aposentar e continuar a servir a como pastor e missionario da igreja Luterana de todas formas possíveis. Depois de sua morte, minha avó continuou a viver nesta casa em Missiones por varios anos. Em outubro de 1970 ela mudou-se para os Nova Iorque, nos EUA, onde viveu com sua filha Monica, onde veio a falecer no dia 17 de Fevereiro de 1986. Ela foi sepultada ao lado do seu filho Reginald, em Fayetteville, no estado da Carolina do Norte, EUA, e seu neto, o Rev. Walter Lehenbauer oficiou seu enterro.

Já havia mencionado que os dois irmãos do pastor Albert, Conrad e George, também foram pastores no Brasil. Além disto, uma de suas irmãs, Anna, casou-se com o pastor Edwin Fisher e se mudou para Australia. Mas entre os filhos do pastor Albert Lehenbauer, somente Reginald se formou pastor, porém exerceu este cargo somente por bem pouco tempo. Tres filhas do pastor Lehenbauer, Naomi, Flora e Monica, se casaram com pastores. E dentre todos os netos do pastor Albert eu sou o único que se formou pastor, coisa que ja faço desde Janeiro de 1982.

Em 1981, quando tive a oportunidade de passar férias no Brasil, meus pais e eu fizemos uma viagem a Santa Rosa e de lá para Linha 15, ou seja, Urwahnfried. Durante esta viagem meu pai me contou muitas coisas da sua infância. Na época, inclusive, chegamos a visitar a casa pastoral onde ele passou seu primeiors 14 anos de vida. Esta casa pastoral era imensa, e por este motivo foi apelidada de "Elefante Branco." Algumas coisas na casa me chamaram atenção. Meu avô fala neste livrinho a respeito dos buracos que fez no assoalho para deixar a água das chuvas torrenciais escorrer pra fora, coisa que eu pessoalmente achei engraçado, pois não creio que esta solução seria a primeira escolha de qualquer dona de casa, mas enfim, foi a solução que ele encontrou. Outra coisa muito curiosa foi que ao subir para o segundo andar da casa, eu me surpreendi ao ver uma torneira a meio caminho da escada. Ao perguntar a meu pai porque havia uma torneira justamente ali, ele disse que o meu avô havia colocado esta torneira ali para facilitar a limpeza do andar superior, pois trazer baldes de água do andar de baixo era um sacrifício. Assim ele instalou um assim chamado "carneiro" hidráulico há uma boa distância da casa, que trazia água para o andar térreo, mas infelizmente não havia jeito de ter água no andar de cima. Instalando a torneira no meio da subida da escada, na maneira de pensar dele, era portanto, uma grande coisa para facilitar o trabalho de manter a casa limpa. Ao me levar à parte de cima da casa, meu pai apontou para janela que ficava na cabeceira de sua cama, quando este era seu quarto de guri. Ele me disse que o vô muitas vezes vinha ficar junto com seus filhos em noites de temporais com muitos relampagos. Ao ver seus filhos tremerem de medo dos fortes estrondos, ele dizia que deveriam se concentrar no que viam à distância, no horizonte. Era como um fotógrafo, dizia ele, que tirando uma foto com flash, fazia com que se pudesse ver instantaneamente o que estava sendo fotografado. Desta maneira, meu vô ensinou seus filhos a não ter medo de temporais. Muitos anos mais tarde, quando meu pai em noites escuras de temporal e cheias de relampagos via seus cinco filhos tremerem de medo com os estrondos dos relampagos, ele também os levava à janela do seu quarto e dizia que deveriam imaginar que tudo aquilo era como um fotógrafo, que tirando fotos instantaneas, gravando em filme o que estava diante dele. Ao mesmo tempo meu pai nos incentivava a nos concentrar no que viamos no instante do relampago, isto é: a figura de um cavalo, uma nuvem, o mato ou uma árvore em frente a nossa casa, etc. Isto se tornou como uma brincadeira e mal percebemos, que ao passar dos anos, ja não pecisávamos de nosso pai ao nosso lado, pois perdemos o medo dos relampagos e fortes temporais com o uso do mesmo estratagema usado por meu avô, em decadas anteriores.

Fiquei muito surpreso ao coversar com os filhos e netos dos congregandos do meu avô por ocasião da Fenasoja em 2004. Estou bem lembrado que um senhor de grande idade fez questão de me dar a mão e pedir que me sentasse ao seu lado para conversar, o que eu fiz com todo gosto. No decorrer da conversa, ele me disse que era menino quando o avô Albert deixou o Brasil para ir à Argentina. Como o avô adorava música clássica, e sua obra favorita era a 9 sinfonia de Behthoven, este senhor tocou parte desta obra no seu violino e a escola cantou esta música na sua festa de despedida. Ele também mencionou que muitos dos congregandos por gostarem tanto do seu pastor, começaram a nomear seus próprios filhos com os mesmos nomes que meus avós haviam escolhido para suas crianças, coisa que eu nunca havia ouvido antes. Foi ai que ele me disse que ele era o "tocaio" do meu pai, pois tinha o mesmo nome (Siegfried). Uma senhora de idade bastante avançada, que só falava alemão, me disse que se lembrava muito bem do pastor Lehenbauer, pois ele a havia confirmado. Desde então, para ela, não havia outro pastor que chegasse nem perto dele, ao seu modo de ver e entender o pastorado. Muitos outros filhos de membros, cujos nomes não lembro mais, me disseram que seus pais sempre falavam muito a respeito do pastor Lehenbauer, pois ele tinha uma maneira toda especial de trazer cultura e progresso aos seus congregandos. Todo mundo fala da introdução da soja, o que é sem dúvida uma grande coisa, pois mudou para melhor a vida dos colonos em Urwahnfried, e depois, em todo o Brasil. Mas, me disseram estas pessoas, poucos falam das outras coisas que o seu pastor fez por seus congregandos. Como lia e viajava muito, falando com todo mundo, por assim dizer, ele sempre sabia das ultimas novidades e tinha conhecimento sobre os últimos descobrimentos científicos. Quando voltava se suas longas e frequentes viagens, não só trazia discos de músicas clássicas para introduzir um nível de cultura bastante incomum aos seus congregandos, mas também trazia outras coisas, que acabavam por facilitar suas vidas. Numa ocasião ele trouxe um touro, ninguém sabe como ou de onde, animal este que ele então emprestava ao seus congregandos para cruzar com suas vacas leiteras para produzir vacas que produziam mais leite. Em outra ocasião ele trouxe (niguém sabe de onde ou como conseguiu fazer isto) uma espécie toda especial de peixes, para estocar açudes, pois muitos dos seus membros não tinham os meios necessários para se alimentar com mais proteina. Estas e muitas outras coisas eu ouvi de várias pessoas na Fenasoja em 2004, que eram crianças quando o pastor Albert aceitou um chamado para Argentina ou, cujos pais eram congregandos do meu avô. Todos estes relatos pessoais me chamaram atenção pois percebi que no fundo tinham a mesma mensagem, isto é: meu avô não so era apenas seu líder espiritual nos fins de semana, mas o seu exemplo de vida era tal que realmente se esmerou em fazer tudo que foi possível para melhorar a vida daqueles colonos, que veio a tratar como seus verdadeiros e amados irmãos na fé em Cristo.

Para ele, as dificuldades que passou durante os seus anos de pastorado no Brasil e na Argentina valeram a pena, pois no final, ele teve a grande alegria dever seus membros terem a oportunidade de crescer e se fortalescer na fé de Cristo. Além disto, pela graça de Deus, ele também pode ajudar a enriquecer suas vidas de maneiras muito variadas, assim como introduzindo-os à música clássica e à leitura de autores famosos, além de contribuir para mudar seu poder aquisitivo e melhorar a sua maneira de viver. Por isto mesmo penso que se meu avô pudesse ver o que aconteceu em Urwahnfried, especialmente nestas últimas décadas, creio que ele ficaria muito surpreso com o progresso econômico da região. Ao mesmo tempo, creio que uma coisa que chamaria a sua atenção sobremaneira é o fato que os seus congregados realmente tem muitas razões diferentes para serem agredecidos a Deus por tudo que Ele permitiu acontecer nas suas vidas, especialmente nestas últimas décadas. Soli Deo Gloria.

Rev. Walter Lehenbauer
Cloquet, Minnesota, EUA

Introdução Histórica

O REV. ALBERT ERNST HEINRICH LEHENBAUER nasceu em 13 de fevereiro de 1891, em West Ely, Missouri (EUA). Foi enviado pela LCMS como missionário ao Brasil em 1914. Aqui se estabeleceu em Santa Rosa (hoje Ubiretama), onde casou-se com Helena Priebe e teve oito filhos. Fundou, juntamente com líderes locais, a União Colonial da Linha 23 de Julho, onde incentivava, nos encontros com os líderes, além do estudo da Palavra, o cultivo da soja e outras práticas agrícolas.

E esse pastor Albert Lehenbauer foi um instrumento de Deus, não só para manter a fé desses imigrantes luteranos que precisavam de assistência espiritual, mas também, melhorar a vida dos agricultores que viviam com grandes dificuldades e com poucas escolas, poucos recursos técnicos para atuar na área agrícola.

Assim ele resolve trazer dos Estados Unidos, em uma de suas viagens de férias, um punhado de sementes de soja, as quais ele distribuiu entre os colonos que participavam de seus estudos bíblicos. E, com isto, não só encontrou uma alternativa de sobrevivência da sociedade que o rodeava, mas a encontrar soluções, estabelecendo uma revolução agrícola. E se tornou o mais importante agente de transformação na história da cidade, a partir do ano de 1924. Mais do que sua atividade fiel como missionário da LCMS, como pastor e educador, ele também usou suas outras qualificações, na educação e agricultura e colocou tudo isso a disposição para servir seus congregados.

Ele, com sua atuação na sociedade, se tornou o protagonista de benefício do bem-estar social daquela sociedade na qual se inseriu. Não foi um mero espectador. O Pastor Albert, foi um líder de transformação, inspirou novos projetos, fortaleceu parcerias e incrementou uma agricultura diferenciada em todo o país. Com a sua ação foi um instrumento de mudança que impactou aquela sociedade até os dias de hoje.

Em novembro de 2024, quando foram celebrados na Fenasoja (Feira Nacional da Soja) em Santa Rosa, os 100 anos da soja no Brasil, esse pastor foi o personagem principal dessa linda história de missão e transformação.

Trabalhou 23 anos aqui no Brasil. Depois aceitou chamado para a Argentina, onde continuou na missão!

Rev. Mario Lehenbauer, Pastor Emérito
Igreja Evangélica Luterana do Brasil

ABRINDO FRONTEIRAS PARA CRISTO NAS SELVAS DO BRASIL

FOI HÁ OITO ANOS ATRÁS QUE O REV. C. TRUNOW e eu navegamos de Nova Iorque a bordo do *S.S. Vasari* em direção aos nossos respectivos campos de missão na América do Sul. Ele estava indo para a Argentina, eu tinha um chamado do Brasil. A viagem marítima até o Rio de Janeiro, de onde nos separaríamos, foi amena e ensolarada. Mas depois disso, as coisas se complicaram. Na alfândega descobri que não tinha nem a metade do dinheiro para pagar o imposto devido. Felizmente o Pastor Trunow pode emprestar-me a quantia faltante necessária.

No porto de Santos, conhecido por sua exportação de café, quase fui deixado para trás, devido ao fato de que o horário de partida do meu navio, um transatlântico costeiro, havia sido antecipado na minha ausência, sem meu conhecimento ou consentimento. Gastei meu último dinheiro de papel para alugar um barco a remo. Mas consegui ultrapassar o navio a vapor. Essa ação do capitão, que considerei uma grande grosseria contra minha digna pessoa, tornou impossível, por falta de fundos, comprar qualquer lanche durante os quatro dias restantes da viagem. Ah, as belas bananas, laranjas, cocos e abacaxis que não pude comprar! Mas isso não foi um infortúnio comparado ao que teria sido se eu tivesse perdido meu navio a vapor.

Não tive oportunidade de escrever, nem dinheiro para telegrafar a data de minha chegada aos irmãos no sul do Brasil, e eu sabia que não haveria ninguém para me receber no cais. Desembarcamos em Porto Alegre, a capital do Rio Grande do Sul, que é o estado mais sulino da República do Brasil, em um feriado, e encontrei a maioria dos estabelecimentos comerciais fechados. Naquela época, nosso seminário estava escondido em um subúrbio discreto, e tive dificuldade em obter qualquer informação a respeito dele: Três vezes, e de três direções totalmente diferentes, fui enviado para um e o mesmo era um seminário católico. Ao meio-dia, almocei deliciosas uvas, que comprei com minhas últimas moedas (tendo separado o suficiente para a passagem), e por meio da linguagem de sinais, pois eu não tinha a menor ideia de que em português, a língua do país, elas têm o mesmo nome que em latim, "uva". Eu também não sabia se as estava comprando por peso, unidade ou a esmo. Por fim, depois de carregar minha bagagem de mão por cinco horas, encontrei um alemão que já havia ouvido um de nossos professores pregar e que pode me indicar o caminho para o nosso seminário.

Depois de alguns dias agradáveis com os irmãos em Porto Alegre, fiz uma breve visita a cada um de meus dois irmãos que haviam entrado no trabalho missionário brasileiro cerca de um ano antes de mim. Em seguida, embarquei no 'pequeno trem da não extensa ferrovia brasileira', com destino ao meu próprio campo missionário. Guarani é o seu nome e, por um descuido dos cartógrafos, o nome não se encontra na maioria dos mapas. Você não o encontrará no seu. Da minha parte, eu preferiria que o Polo Norte, que não tem utilidade alguma para ninguém, tivesse sido omitido dos atlas, pois Guarani para algumas pessoas, inclusive para mim, é o centro da terra.

Depois de dois dias de enjoo constante na ferrovia de bitola estreita, muito curvilínea e muito instável, cheguei à cidade de Ijuí, na época o ponto terminal da estrada de ferro, onde fui recebido pelo Rev. Emil Muller. 97 quilômetros ainda me separavam do destino das minhas esperanças e expectativas. Era um trecho de estradas rurais que deveríamos percorrer em uma charrete que havia sido trazida para o Rev. Muller. Em consequência das chuvas fortes, o tempo normal de 16 horas para essa distância se transformou em três dias inteiros. No primeiro dia andamos ao longo do quase concluído leito em construção para a continuação da estrada de ferro, à qual acrescentei descontraidamente o pronome possessivo da primeira pessoa do singular, chamando-a "minha estrada de ferro". No segundo e terceiro dias, meu ânimo foi mantido pelo Rev. Muller, que alegremente repetia: "Quando tivermos conquistado esta colina à nossa frente, estaremos bem mais perto do que estamos agora". Essa mesma certeza me serviu muito bem em meu trabalho mais tarde, quando a estrada era muito íngreme e ainda por cima enlameada.

Finalmente, subimos a última colina. Estávamos em Guarani (ou Guarany). Pronuncie "gwah-rah-nee," ênfase na última sílaba. Esse "y" final em tantas palavras sul-americanas é uma palavra indígena para "água" ou "rio". Mas Guarani, na verdade, não é o nome de um rio, mas o de uma grande colonização apadrinhada pelo Governo do Estado do Rio Grande do Sul. Dessa grande colônia eu estava interessado apenas em uma pequena parte, colonizada quase exclusivamente por russos alemães. Tente imaginar um enorme pedaço de cuca com cerca de 25 metros de comprimento e 12 quilômetros de largura. A parte do topo da cuca é pura e ininterrupta floresta brasileira primitiva, composta de árvores com troncos distorcidos e uma densa vegetação rasteira de cipós, arbustos, bambus, samambaias, etc. Agora imagine-se cortando essa cuca longitudinalmente em tiras de 2 quilômetros de largura. Desculpe-me por sobrecarregar sua mente com essas frações, mas é assim pelo fato de que o governo brasileiro usa o sistema métrico de pesos e medidas. Gostaria que fosse assim também nos Estados Unidos. Onde a faca passou ao cortar a cuca, imaginaremos um caminho para passar a cavalo, em muitos lugares até mesmo fechados no topo pelos galhos densos das árvores e os cipós que crescem nelas. Mais tarde, essas trilhas serão ampliadas e se tornarão estradas para carroças e automóveis. Algumas das mais importantes já podiam ser usadas para o tráfego de carroças quando eu cheguei. Agora, por favor, um corte no meio da cuca, convertendo cada tira longa em duas mais curtas. Essa é a nossa única encruzilhada, e uma encruzilhada ruim, pois a maioria dos tocos parece ter escolhido seus lugares na estrada e não ao lado dela; e a única vala de drenagem corre exatamente no centro da estrada. De vez em quando você se depara com um buraco de lama e não sabe se vai andar, nadar, pular ou voar. Recentemente, em 1921, ouvi um caso em que o cavalo de um imigrante desapareceu repentina e completamente em um buraco e por pouco não se afogou. A incerteza, no entanto, não é culpa do buraco, mas sim vem da sua inexperiência. Você ainda é "lenha verde" quando se trata de estradas brasileiras. Já vai saber porque!

Agora dividimos cada um dos nossos dois pedaços de cuca em duas partes mais estreitas por um corte no meio, que não é uma estrada ou caminho, mas apenas uma linha divisória. Depois cortamos as partes em pedaços de pouco mais de 800 metros de comprimento e 250 metros de largura. Esses trechos, contendo cerca de 62 acres de mata são os "lotes rurais" ou fazendas dos imigrantes, vendidas a eles em termos muito favoráveis pelo governo estadual por cerca de 125 dólares americanos. Além do mais, como os imigrantes foram transportados de seus antigos lares para o novo local pelo governo federal brasileiro, esse não era um mau negócio de forma alguma. A maioria das fazendas tinha água corrente na forma de uma nascente, um riacho ou um rio.

Quando falamos de russos alemães, estamos nos referindo a pessoas de origem puramente alemã, que, no entanto, foram habitantes da Rússia por uma ou mais gerações. Das suas colônias alemãs preservadas mais ou menos puras na Rússia, eles preservaram a maioria das características físicas, mentais e culturais—características trazidas da Alemanha há uma ou mais gerações atrás. Tendo em mente o seu idioma e costumes, às vezes me lembro de coisas que li sobre como era a vida nas colônias alemãs há cerca de cem anos ou mais. Isso inclui algumas qualidades muito boas e outras ruins. Entre elas, a propensão a mentir e roubar absorvidas das vizinhas culturas russa e polonesa.

Quase todos eles são trabalhadores da madeira no sentido mais abrangente do termo, sendo capazes de produzir uma variedade notável de artigos de madeira somente com as árvores da floresta e algumas ferramentas simples a seu serviço. Já os vi cortar os mais longos peitoris perfeitamente retos sem uma linha de giz; eles serram suas tábuas à mão com bastante rapidez e gostam do trabalho; fazem o melhor tipo de polimento de madeira com pouquíssimo aparato e sem vernizes. Se alguém em algum momento foi colocado nas terras mais adequada às suas necessidades particulares, foram esses imigrantes russo-alemães que chegaram ao Brasil nos últimos dez anos antes da grande guerra. Gostaria de poder dizer com sinceridade que todos eles são gratos por isso, e pelo clima subtropical agradável e saudável, e por terem sido poupados dos horrores daquela catástrofe mundial.

Nessa cuca, colonizada por quase mil famílias de imigrantes, eu deveria assumir o meu campo missionário, para bem ou para mal. Eu tinha certeza de que seria para melhor, e gostava da metáfora da floresta virgem e do solo virgem aplicada ao tema da igreja e da educação escolar. Mas não levou muito tempo para descobrir que eu teria algumas soleiras para cortar e algumas tábuas para serrar em meu trabalho missionário. Mas por que falar em trabalho missionário? Eram essas pessoas pagãs?

De nome, eram luteranos. Mas, na maioria dos casos, seu luteranismo terminava com o nome e as certidões de batismo e outros certificados que traziam consigo. A chamada igreja luterana da Rússia antes da guerra sofria de todas as doenças das igrejas estatais unidas da Alemanha e tinha uma ou duas doenças a mais: Não era a pior delas o fato de que os pastores às vezes eram forçados a dar Santa Ceia aos luteranos à maneira luterana e então comungar os membros da igreja reformada em sua própria tradição no mesmo altar. Pior ainda era o fato de que os pastores eram, em primeiro lugar e principalmente, funcionários do governo russo, tendo como principal dever a manutenção dos registros que serviam de base para os alistamentos militares, e somente em segundo lugar eram pastores do rebanho de Cristo. Além disso, na maioria dos casos eles estavam tão sobrecarregados de congregações que raramente conseguiam visitá-las mais de uma ou duas vezes por ano, embora dessem dois cultos cada dia da semana, enquanto visitando suas paroquias. Quando eles vinham, estavam tão sobrecarregados com afazeres rotineiros que o trabalho principal de um pastor, a alimentação de almas imortais com a pregação da Palavra, recebia apenas uma parte muito pequena de sua atenção e de suas forças físicas. Estava fora de questão instruir pessoalmente suas centenas de catecúmenos. Muitos deles viam o seu pastor pela primeira vez na vida no dia da confirmação. É muito duvidoso que, em média, o pastor tenha chegado a conhecer pessoalmente até mesmo um por cento de seus paroquianos, seja no momento da confirmação ou na vida do além.

Normalmente o culto dominical consistia na leitura de um sermão por aquele a quem chamavam de professor, que também tomava o lugar do pastor na instrução dos jovens e em grande parte do trabalho pastoral na maioria das congregações: A maior parte desses professores não tinha treinamento algum, era incapaz de expor as principais doutrinas da fé cristã e geralmente se contentava em fazer com que os seus confirmandos memorizassem as partes principais do Catecismo de maneira mais ou menos defeituosa. Longe de escrever qualquer livro, os pastores nem mesmo supriam a falta de livros luteranos importando-os da Alemanha ou dos Estados Unidos. O suprimento de livros foi deixado nas mãos dos judeus. É verdade que havia pouco interesse em bons livros. Mas não eram exatamente os pastores que deveriam ter criado esse interesse? E será que o interesse não teria crescido se o suprimento de livros tivesse sido providenciado? Alguns dos filhos mais jovens do Sínodo de Missouri não tiveram a oportunidade de apreciar o que temos disponível em nosso esplêndido acervo de bons e interessantes livros e periódicos, e muitos de nós são tão ingratos quanto os nove leprosos, porque não os lemos como deveríamos.

Nessas condições, na Rússia, muitas dessas crianças russas alemãs, filhos de Deus por seu batismo, cresceram sem realmente entender as doutrinas principais da sua fé, sem saber por que eram chamadas de luteranos. É verdade que tiveram muitos bons sermões luteranos lidos para eles em seus lugares de reunião (que eles chamam de "escolas", mas que nem sempre eram usadas para fins escolares); mas eles não tinham a chave para entender esses sermões, pois mal entendiam sua linguagem e, portanto, pouco ou nada aproveitavam deles. E assim, muitos deles haviam crescido dentro da igreja luterana visível, permanecendo nela por tradição e por uma certa pressão exercida pelo Estado, mas pagãos em seus corações, não acreditando que a Bíblia é a palavra de Deus e não querendo ser governados por ela.

Não é fácil para mim escrever isso. Não foi fácil nem mesmo acreditar nisso. Mas meu objetivo atual é não encobrir, mas dizer a verdade ao pintar o pano de fundo do meu trabalho. Eu me propus a demonstrar por que falamos de missão entre os chamados luteranos. E na época da minha chegada a Guarani, um número deplorável dessas mil famílias havia comprovado a veracidade do que escrevi. Centenas tinham ido para a igreja batista, porque tinham sido facilmente persuadidos de que sua fé luterana era uma fé sem obras e, portanto, morta. Centenas de outros sentiram a diminuição dos grilhões do controle estatal e, consequentemente, abandonaram a influência dos bons costumes, que sentiam igualmente como opressiva, e agora estavam mostrando que eram realmente pagãos, cem por cento pagãos.

E aqui estava eu, disposto a me familiarizar com esse tipo de gente tão interessante, embora nem sempre agradável. Antes mesmo de eu chegar, no entanto, Deus já havia construído uma escola especial com o propósito de me ajudar nos primeiros passos de meu trabalho. Não havia uma casa pastoral pronta para mim, mas me ofereceram sem custo uma pequena casa vazia como minha primeira residência temporária. Era parte de um antigo moinho de água. Quando entrei no pátio do moinho, localizado em um vale isolado, o moleiro—meu futuro professor—estava na porta de entrada. Seu nome era Mertens, e era um homem muito peculiar. Temo que, apesar da sua recepção amigável, a primeira impressão não me proporcionou a sensação de alívio e prazer que sinto agora quando penso nele. Era corcunda e dois acidentes físicos quase fatais nos melhores anos da sua vida o condenaram a ser chamado por todos que o conheciam de "o velho Mertens". Mas logo comecei a sentir o frescor que emana de uma alma grande e maravilhosa. Ele não tinha nenhuma educação escolar. Era tão ingênuo quanto a maioria de seus compatriotas em termos de leis e regras gramaticais. Mas ele lê, fala e escreve em quatro idiomas, sem contar o iídiche, do qual também é mestre. Às vezes, palavras longas saíam atravessadas, ou com uma sílaba suprimida ou invertida. Mas, com a vantagem de não ter que se preocupar com a sua forma, ele captava perfeitamente o sentido delas. Sua memória é um milagre para mim, e ele parece nunca ter se esquecido de nada que tenha visto, ouvido ou lido. O que tinha lido teria enchido uma boa prateleira de pelo menos um metro e meio—e incluía meia dúzia de volumes da edição de St. Louis de Lutero. Um fluxo incessante de humor espontâneo, uma piedade genuína sem pietismo e uma boa reputação entre amigos e inimigos eram a coroa gloriosa de sua personalidade singular.

Em seu moinho, ele tinha o que ele mesmo chama de um pequeno posto missionário. Com um coração tão cheio de fé, não poderia ser diferente. Apenas melhora uma boa oportunidade, pois ao seu moinho vêm os representantes de todas as tendências religiosas para ter seu milho moído. E enquanto os seus grãos caíam entre as pedras do moinho, geralmente os pensamentos mais íntimos de todos esses corações estavam sendo moídos entre as pedras da mente poderosa do moleiro. Isso era tão natural e um processo tão completo e indolor que eu, que adoro tomar a conversa em minhas próprias mãos em outras ocasiões, me senti feliz em sentar quase inebriado em um saco de grãos, às vezes por horas a fio, ouvindo e apreciando, e aprendendo como nunca havia aprendido aos pés dos meus bons professores. Aprendi a entender e a falar o tipo específico de alemão que essas pessoas usam, familiarizei-me completamente com os lados bons e ruins de seu caráter, aprendi a ver o lado bom sob a casca áspera quando havia uma boa semente sob a casca bruta; tornei-me completamente familiarizado com os truques e argumentos usados pelos vários inimigos do verdadeiro luteranismo, e tive algumas armas poderosas contra eles colocadas nas minhas mãos pelo "velho" moleiro-teólogo; fiz um curso completo de pós-graduação na aplicação de nossa doutrina luterana às novas condições especiais que estavam me confrontando no meu trabalho.

No início, eu aprendia apenas ouvindo, mas depois de alguns meses comecei a participar da conversa, fazendo os necessários exercícios práticos sob a supervisão do meu professor. Nessas ocasiões, depois que o freguês do moinho tinha ido embora, eu perguntava ao moleiro-missionário se minha linguagem tinha sido clara e se os meus argumentos foram compreendidos por aqueles a quem se destinavam; e ele sempre respondia com absoluta franqueza quais das minhas palavras e frases tinham sido "gramaticais demais" para o ouvinte. Recebi meu diploma no final do meu primeiro ano, quando após um debate com um inimigo eminente que durou das 7 da manhã às 7 da noite, sem um intervalo sequer para beber um copo de água, no qual o meu professor já não quis participar (e foi uma prova de seu maravilhoso tato que ele não o tenha feito), mas se limitou a prover alguns testemunhos luteranos, quando, depois desse debate, ele espontaneamente disse que agora eu estava sendo compreendido pelos meus ouvintes. Senti mais alegria ao receber esse diploma do que os dois diplomas de latim que tinha recebido anteriormente.

Entre o moinho e a casa onde moro, há uma cozinha antiga, um pequeno barraco de madeira sem piso, com portas maltratadas e janelas sem caixilhos e venezianas, e a metade de uma parede enegrecida pelo fogo. Diante dessa parede, um arame pendia de uma viga, segurando na extremidade inferior um velho caldeirão preto de ferro fundido sobre um fogo aberto e, ao redor do fogo, estava nossa matilha de cães e gatos, que vigiavam a chaleira e se aqueciam no calor. Aqueles que tiveram o privilégio de conhecer os encantos secretos dessa antiga cozinha ainda falam dela como "a cozinha enfeitiçada". Mas naquele caldeirão não borbulhava mingau de mendigo, nem caldo encantado de bruxa. Dentro dele eram colocados cada manhã nossa porção diária de feijão preto brasileiro e bacon defumado ou costelinha. E todo meio-dia, quando o estômago começava a se fazer ouvir naquela linguagem inconfundível, a boia estava deliciosamente pronta para ser transferida do caldeirão para o prato dos esfomeados. Oh, como aquela mesma sensação de fome volta à minha mente aqui na bela Nova Iorque, em meio a essa variedade desconcertante de coisas boas para comer, só de pensar naqueles almoços e jantas de feijão todos os dias, um presente de Deus para o Brasil! E o nosso jeito de comer era tão simples e confortável! O Mertens era apenas um inquilino, com sua família morando em seu próprio "lote rural", não muito longe do moinho. Éramos um lar sem mãe. Portanto, nunca comíamos à mesa, até mesmo porque não tínhamos nenhuma, mas todo mundo vinha e enchia seu prato quando estivesse pronto. E todo mundo escolhia a posição que mais lhe agradava, em pé, sentado ou reclinado em estilo clássico.

Isso me faz lembrar de uma cena que vi naquela velha cozinha enfeitiçada que poderia valer um milhão se fosse pintada. Tivemos um convidado, nascido em Leipzig, mas formado em nosso seminário em Porto Alegre, o Rev. Raschke. Um dia ele chegou primeiro do que eu na panela de carne e feijão. Quando entrei na cozinha, ele, baixinho e corcunda, já estava sentado lá, em um banco baixo, com o precioso prato de feijão sobre os joelhos. Bem diante dele estava nosso querido cãozinho Wackerlos, com seu nariz bem treinado e gracioso logo abaixo da borda do prato (uma contenção natural, já que ele não tinha comprimento corporal para chegar mais perto do prato). Atrás e acima dele estava o nosso grande, magro, e apenas meio civilizado Gaspodin Brasovitch, com seu focinho bárbaro erguido da forma mais impropria acima da borda do prato. Sob o braço direito do Raschke, a nossa venerável gata mãe, de cabelos grisalhos, insinuando-se e se deliciando com o cheiro do feijão. E sob o braço esquerdo, nossa melindrosa gata Narcissa, nascida na mansão, com pelo menos três gerações da cultura local em seu sangue, deleitava o seu nariz pequeno e bem torneado no perfume do bacon. Lá estava o Raschke desenvolvendo o seu caráter e melhorando o seu homem interior, como diria o Mertens! Se houve um momento na minha vida em que me arrependi de não ter uma câmera em condições de funcionamento comigo, foi esse!

A casa perto do antigo moinho foi o ponto de partida para minhas viagens aos diferentes pontos de pregação. No início eram dezessete postos missionários. Além dos treze da região da "cuca", havia mais quatro a uma distância de 8 a 20 horas de sela. Essas horas correspondem a cerca de quatro quilômetros cada. Em tempo chuvoso, leva-se muito mais do uma hora para percorrer essa distância. Durante o meu primeiro ano, praticamente gastei dois cavalos, estando na estrada em média cinco dias por semana, na maior parte das vezes da manhã até quase meia-noite. Depois de perder um terceiro cavalo por uma troca não intencional e infeliz, que deixou nas minhas mãos um cavalo desgastado e ossudo, que pode ter sido um primo em primeiro grau do Spark Plug da famosa coluna de humor do jornal, resolvi desistir dos cavalos. Tive a sorte de conseguir duas "Missouri"-mulas grandes e finas importadas da República do Uruguai. Elas eram totalmente indomadas e tinham um medo mortal de qualquer homem exceto um negro. Mas os domadores de cavalos negros e brasileiros também tinham medo de mulas, e eu não queria que elas fossem domadas se primeiro tivessem que passar fome até quase à morte, o que é uma prática comum. Uma vez nós as atrelamos a um vagão carregado de madeira, na companhia de outras mulas, e então os meninos do Mertens as montaram pela primeira vez. Depois disso elas foram colocadas a serviço da missão, embora isso significasse colocar minha vida em risco cada vez que eu montava nos animais meio domesticados. Mas depois que elas se familiarizaram comigo e desenvolvi uma forma de lidar com elas, eu tinha nas mãos dois animais de carga insubstituíveis e não os trocaria pela melhor meia dúzia de cavalos do Kentucky.

Essas viagens em lombo de mula foram, em sua maioria, interessantes, o que não significa, entretanto, que tenham sido agradáveis. Logo após a chegada das mulas, também me mudei para a casa paroquial que, na época, estava quase na metade. Dali, um dia fui chamado para batizar uma criança em um lugar a oito quilômetros de distância. Não havia lamaçais na estrada, mas a estrada inteira era um único buraco de lama até os joelhos. Isso significava ir a pé o caminho todo. Após o batismo, a mãe da criança desejou ser comungada. Eu não havia levado vinho, e não havia nenhum mais perto do que da casa paroquial. Não havia ninguém para mandar buscar vinho, ou melhor, não havia cavalo para alguém montar. Portanto, não havia mais nada a fazer do que voltar caminhando e buscar os elementos necessários. Quando saí novamente daquela casa após a comunhão, o sol estava se pondo. Mas havia um casamento anunciado para a tarde. Para evitar qualquer decepção, eu havia deixado um aviso para que o casal se dirigisse à casa dos pais da noiva imediatamente depois do casamento civil, prometendo chegar lá assim que possível. Para me poupar de uns quilômetros de estradas ruins, peguei um novo caminho, que, no entanto, já havia sido usada tempo suficiente para transformar-se no mesmo lamaçal até os joelhos. Era uma noite escura. Aquela trilha, que era coberta por vegetação densa, estava tão escura quanto um túnel de pedra sólida. Somente pelo ruído dos pés da mula contra o barro era possível saber que eu ainda estava na estrada. Eu estava em estado de alerta máximo, pois não queria ter o meu crânio batendo contra algum galho enorme ou um de meus globos oculares contra a extremidade saliente e afiada de algum broto de bambu. E eu sabia por experiência própria que qualquer ruído incomum, como o crepitar de um caniço quebrado, faria com que minha jovem mula, assustada, disparasse para salvar a sua vida. O pior que aconteceu por um longo tempo foi ter o meu chapéu arrancado da minha cabeça por um galho, e aí ter que procurá-lo no escuro. E assim eu cavalguei, cavalguei e cavalguei, e continuei cavalgando. Algumas coisas se expandem com o calor, mas quilômetros se expandem com a escuridão. De repente, minha mula estava de pé nas suas patas traseiras e girava em torno de mim, como um pião. Eu não podia fazer nada para detê-la. Então fiz a melhor coisa que poderia ter feito naquele momento: sentei na sela e esperei, sabendo que ela não poderia girar a noite toda. E assim foi. Quando ela parou, eu me desvencilhei das ramas e desci. Uma árvore havia caído no caminho. Eu supus que já houvesse um caminho de emergência para contornar a obstrução e tentei levar minha mula até lá. Ela se recusou a ser guiada na escuridão. Eu a amarrei numa árvore e encontrei o atalho caindo na lama e ensopando minhas botas. Fiquei feliz até com isso. Voltei para a mula, montei na sela e cavalguei. Mas quando cheguei lá, eu absolutamente não sabia nada sobre os caminhos que havia percorrido. Não sabia onde havia estado, nem a direção em que estava indo. Por um bom tempo, sentado na sela, pensei e pensei. Nenhum resultado. Pensei intensamente. Nenhum resultado ainda. Pensei ainda mais. Resultado: Um raio de luz naquela escuridão assustadora: "Apenas um caminho pode estar errado, então o outro deve estar certo". Segui. E eu cavalguei, cavalguei e cavalguei, e ainda cavalguei. Então veio o primeiro raio de luz física. Cheguei a uma estrada mais larga, aberta encima. Eu me achei . . . reconheci o lugar por um grande tronco na beira da estrada. Eu estava de volta ao lugar onde tinha visto o pôr do sol. O que poderia fazer senão respirar fundo, relaxar e seguir pelo caminho mais longo, passando pela casa pastoral? Finalmente, um pouco antes da meia-noite, cheguei à casa da noiva e encontrei o futuro marido dormindo profundamente em decorrência de bebidas e da longa espera, e realizei a cerimônia de casamento entre interrupções pelos convidados bêbados.

Em outra ocasião, comprei vários mapas para minhas escolas em Ijuí. Para ter certeza de que eles chegariam em casa secos, eu os embrulhei em minha capa de chuva e os enviei com um motorista. Era um belo e ensolarado dia de inverno. Eu pretendia fazer um caminho de ida e volta, aumentando a distância para 20 horas. Mas eu pretendia percorrer essa distância sem parar, viajando a noite toda para não perder a hora da aula de catecismo em casa. No final da tarde, começou a chuviscar e quanto mais escuro ficava, mais forte chovia, e quanto mais chovia, mais frio ficava. E eu, coitado, só com uma roupa de montaria cáqui! Por volta das sete horas da tarde, nós, ou seja, eu e a mula, caímos numa vala. Sempre afirmei que isso foi intencional por parte da mula. Mas não queria me arriscar novamente. Com a ajuda da iluminação momentânea de um raio, escolhi um arbusto de espinhos para me abrigar. Não que estivesse chovendo menos intensamente ali, mas ainda assim há uma certa sensação de proteção debaixo de um arbusto, no meio da vasta planície sob chuva, raios e trovões. Para não me cansar, me apoiei primeiro sobre a minha perna do lado leste e depois mudei para a minha perna do lado oeste. A mula fez mais ou menos o mesmo. Depois de quase doze horas dessa mudança, amanheceu, e a chuva diminuiu e finalmente parou. O sol quente começou a trabalhar nas minhas roupas molhadas e, quando cheguei em casa depois de mais dez horas na sela, não precisei temer uma bronca por ter molhado minhas belas roupas. Até encontrei uma longa barra de ferro na estrada, peguei-a e a devolvi ao motorista que a havia perdido, deixando-o muito feliz.

Treze postos de pregação em meu entorno imediato eram oito a mais do que deveriam ser. O fato de existirem (além de várias escolas da Igreja Unida) se devia ao fato de que as pessoas haviam sido governadas com a mão de ferro do estado quando ainda estavam na Rússia e, portanto, sabiam pouco sobre a administração prática das congregações bem como da mesma maneira sabiam pouco sobre a doutrina. Além disso, havia a falta de cruzamentos no novo assentamento. A densa floresta virgem formava uma parede natural que dividia em três congregações o que deveria ter sido uma só congregação. Logo percebi que, ao pregar em tantos lugares, eu estava apenas desgastando minhas forças físicas e mentais. Em geral, eu só conseguia pregar uma vez a cada quatro a seis meses, contando com os domingos chuvosos, o que não era muito melhor do que os pastores na Rússia estavam fazendo. E entre minhas poucas e esparsas visitas, a boa semente da palavra teria sido facilmente coberta de neve pelo joio de algum falso profeta, que tinha sua oportunidade uma ou duas vezes por semana.

Na velha "cozinha enfeitiçada", cedo estávamos ocupados deliberando sobre as formas e os meios de uma organização mais prática de toda a igreja Luterana dentro da cuca Guarani. A fundação de uma grande congregação central com a sua sede na ou perto da casa paroquial que estava sendo construída pelo Sínodo, e a gradual adição de outras congregações menores ao redor, provavelmente ao redor de quatro, parecia ser o objetivo natural a ser perseguido. A única medida prática que eu poderia tomar enquanto morava no antigo moinho era convocar os presidentes das 13 assim chamadas congregações, a fim de obter o seu consentimento e ganhar o seu apoio pelo plano. Embora isso possa não ter sido totalmente em vão, não posso dizer que tenha trazido muito progresso.

No momento em que passei a residir na meia-terminada casa paroquial, eu estava em condições de prosseguir com outras medidas. A primeira foi organizar o que chamamos de uma escola noturna. Os homens mais jovens e progressistas das diferentes "congregações" eram convidados a se reunir todas as sextas-feiras à noite no escritório do pastor. Estudávamos alemão leitura, ortografia e gramática, e um pouco de português. Tivemos alguns minutos de exercícios parlamentares para nos acostumarmos com presidentes, secretários, chamadas de quórum, moções, momentos de perguntas, e coisas do gênero, que eram ideias bastante novas para a maioria dos membros. Também iniciei a leitura em série de algumas das histórias de Alfred Ira, tratando de alguns dos problemas da vida congregacional de forma tão magistral. Para garantir a presença e a atenção de todos os membros, na medida do possível, tomávamos nosso chá brasileiro durante essas leituras.

Esse chá é composto de folhas e galhos em pó do mate sul-americano ou chá do Paraguai.[1] Esse chá, que é um excelente substituto para o chá oriental quando bebido em uma decocção fraca, é geralmente tomado na América do Sul em uma forma muito mais forte. Uma pequena cabaça ou outro recipiente adequado é preenchido com o pó de chá, deixando espaço de um lado para inserir um tubo de prata com uma espécie de peneira na parte inferior. Em seguida, o espaço restante é preenchido com água quase fervente. A decocção forte resultante é então sugada do tubo. O anfitrião faz o primeiro enchimento e, em seguida, enche novamente a cabaça para cada convidado. A bebida tem um gosto bastante amargo para o novato e o fato de tantas pessoas diferentes sugarem do mesmo tubo pode parecer para o norte-americano comum como uma forma velada de cometer suicídio. Mas em muitas partes da América do Sul esse é um rito sagrado de hospitalidade e, uma vez que você tenha se acostumado com o sabor e cativado pela bebida, não conheço nenhuma outra bebida no mundo que traga consigo a mesma medida de sociabilidade democrática como essa. Não estou defendendo sua introdução no mundo civilizado, pois acho que ela contém demasiado ácido tânico (11%) para ser saudável. Mas nós o introduzimos com um propósito em nossas reuniões e tenho certeza de que ele ajudou a torná-las um sucesso. O principal objetivo da escola era nos familiarizarmos uns com os outros e ter a oportunidade de conversar sobre o plano da organização. Nisso fomos bem-sucedidos. Não apenas alguns dos antigos alunos noturnos são agora os membros mais ativos e com maior entendimento das nossas congregações reorganizadas, mas alguns deles estão servindo como presidentes e secretários.

Em seguida resolvemos o problema do correio e começamos nossa biblioteca circulante. Mesmo depois de terminado o novo trecho da ferrovia ("Minha Ferrovia"), a casa paroquial ficava a 11 horas de viagem da estação mais próxima, quatro horas do posto de correio governamental mais próximo e 3 horas do telefone mais próximo. Frequentemente minha correspondência fazia uma longa e perigosa viagem de ida e volta antes de chegar até mim. E se há uma coisa no mundo que me irrita é um serviço postal ineficiente. Portanto, nada mais natural para mim do que elaborar um plano para um modelo de sistema postal privado, que nos traria nossas correspondências diretamente da agência postal uma vez por semana. Depois de várias experiências, uma das quais descrevi na época no *Atlantic Monthly*, o correio se tornou, como deveria ser, algo sagrado e encantador, e há anos ele chega à casa paroquial todas as sextas-feiras à noite, faça chuva ou faça sol, para ser distribuído a todas as congregações no sábado ou domingo de manhã. No início, os alunos da escola noturna faziam

---

1 O pastor Albert está se referindo aqui ao chimarrão, uma bebida tradicional do sul do Brasil e de outros países da América do Sul. É preparada com a infusão de erva-mate moída, servida com água quente em uma cuia e consumida por meio de uma bomba. Trata-se de uma bebida de grande importância cultural, cujo ritual de preparo e consumo simboliza tradição e companheirismo.

a distribuição, depois os professores. E agora tínhamos uma organização que nos permitiria introduzir bons periódicos e livros nos lares e, mais tarde, realizar várias atividades que serviriam para uma publicidade digna de nossa igreja e trabalho da igreja e da escola. Apesar das medidas de guerra, que nos atrapalhavam, conseguimos introduzir um número razoável de periódicos. E os livros da biblioteca circulante estavam quase sempre "esgotados". Conheço vários jovens que, por não terem tido a oportunidade de ir à escola na sua infância, aprenderam a ler tão bem com essa biblioteca que não tinham medo de pegar livros muito grossos. E os pais que não sabiam ler, agora podiam desfrutar de uma literatura maravilhosa ouvindo-a ser lida por seus filhos.

Mas como a necessidade de escolas de verdade era a maior necessidade de todos, a Conferência de Professores foi a pedra angular de todo nosso trabalho como organização. Um pequeno número dos chamados professores havia sido trazido da Rússia, e eles foram mantidos no cargo e respeitados como uma herança pelas congregações pelo maior tempo possível. Em sua maioria, eles não sabiam nada sobre bons métodos de ensino, sendo a vara o maior auxiliar de professores e alunos. Com o passar dos anos, o suprimento dessa valiosa classe humana se esgotou. Lamentamos o fato de que o Sínodo não tivesse professores para preenchermos as vagas que surgiam. Mas nós não perdemos muito tempo lamentando. Um certo número de jovens que sabiam ler e até escrever foram escolhidos. A maioria deles não teve educação escolar em sua infância. Mas na medida do possível eles estavam dispostos a recuperar o tempo perdido. E eu estava mais do que disposto a dar a eles a oportunidade. Nós nos reuníamos em conferência na casa paroquial todos os sábados. Começamos do início, passando pelas coisas que uma criança deve aprender nas primeiras semanas e meses de sua vida escolar. Isso era necessário não apenas para mostrar aos homens como transmitir esse conhecimento às crianças, mas porque descobri que eles precisavam disso para o próprio bem deles. Por exemplo, um belo dia ficamos surpresos ao descobrir que um dos nossos mais velhos, que havia ensinado na escola por vários anos, não sabia que toda frase deve começar com letra maiúscula. Depois dessa descoberta, eu não deveria ter ficado surpreso ao encontrá-lo escrevendo seu próprio nome "wlAdislaW steinbRennEr". Essa não foi a única descoberta que fiz. Mas logo fizemos progresso. O que antes ia aos trancos e barrancos começou a caminhar em uma direção saudável. Os pais começaram a aguçar os seus ouvidos. Os ocasionais visitantes às escolas notaram que o professor nunca se sentava em sua poltrona (ou seja, na cadeira de madeira dura atrás da escrivaninha), mas ensinava em pé o dia inteiro. Surpreendeu-os o fato de que ele raramente ou nunca usava a vara, exceto para "apontar". Surpreendeu-os ainda mais que as crianças estivessem aprendendo mais sem o uso da vara do que jamais sonharam ser possível antes. Eles ficavam encantados quando seus meninos e meninas traziam para casa fantásticos livros de história e os liam para seus pais de forma quase tão fluente e inteligível quanto o próprio professor ou pastor. Mas o ponto mais alto foi atingido quando assistiam aos exames públicos e viam suas próprias crianças, entre outras coisas, soletrarem as palavras mais difíceis do idioma alemão sem ajuda de livros e da maneira mais pomposa possível. Nem em sonho teriam imaginado ser isso possível na Rússia. E o mesmo com palavras em português. E eles liam e traduziam o português sem piscar.

Notável, o argumento básico dos velhos sábios começou a perder sua força: "Eu não sei ler nem escrever e vim da Rússia para o Brasil; não vejo por que meus filhos deveriam saber mais do que eu." Um ciúme saudável começou a surgir entre os pais: Os filhos do vizinho não podem ler melhor do que os meus; portanto, os meus não podem ir para a escola menos do que os filhos do vizinho. Foi preciso pedir aos pais para não enviarem os seus filhos muito cedo para a escola. No ano passado, seis famílias de uma congregação estavam enviando trinta crianças para a escola. Uma congregação de 28 famílias estava enviando 72 crianças. E foi somente num dia muito chuvoso que o número de alunos não passou de sessenta. Às vezes, em um dia chuvoso, o professor permanecia em casa, pensando que poderia ter um dia de descanso. Mas isso acabava não dando muito certo, pois as crianças iam buscá-lo em casa. Os pais às vezes reclamavam com o pastor que não podiam manter seus filhos em casa quando precisavam deles. Suponho que não preciso dizer que havia alguns pais e algumas crianças que não aderiram a essa onda geral de entusiasmo pela escola.

E então vieram os nossos corais. Deus enviou um homem para a casa paroquial, uma criatura inútil para outras coisas, mas que amava a música, que tinha formação musical e que era dotado de uma bela voz pela graça de Deus. Por vários anos ele controlou as suas más inclinações, entre elas o alcoolismo, a ponto de permitir-lhe reger e inspirar os nossos corais, até que, nos últimos anos, o tempo do pastor permitiu que ele assumisse esse trabalho. Por aproximadamente seis anos, nossos sete corais cantaram centenas das melhores composições do mundo, como as composições corais da *Paixão segundo São Mateus* de Bach, entre outros. Os cantores se mostravam sempre cheios de entusiasmo e mal se davam conta do difícil e esplêndido trabalho que estavam fazendo. Nunca perdemos de vista a meta principal que havíamos estabelecido para nós mesmos: promover o desenvolvimento da organização das congregações por meio de corais. Fizemos isso ao trazer pessoas aos nossos cultos, ao treinar as congregações para cantar nossos esplêndidos corais luteranos clássicos de uma forma original e ao fazer uso dos ensaios para discussões proveitosas sobre desafios congregacionais. Uma observação secundária importante: Conseguimos eliminar os hinos no estilo Moody e Sankey que chegaram até nós em traduções abomináveis, mas eram adorados por suas melodias e ritmos inspiradores.[2]

2 David Sankey (28 de agosto de 1840–13 de agosto de 1908) foi um cantor e compositor de música gospel norte-americano, conhecido por sua longa parceria com Dwight L. Moody (5 de fevereiro de 1837–22 de dezembro de 1899), um evangelista também norte-americano. Juntos, eles realizaram uma série de campanhas de avivamento religioso nos Estados Unidos e na Grã-Bretanha durante as últimas décadas do século XIX. Os hinos

Não foi sem luta que obtivemos esses resultados. Vou mencionar apenas as mais importantes, e muito brevemente. Lutamos contra o "patriotismo local". Todos estavam dispostos a se unir em congregações maiores. Mas todos queriam que a integração se desse nos seus termos: que os outros se adaptassem a nós. "Deve ser na nossa rua, na nossa escola!" Foi contra esse inimigo que nosso canto provou ser uma arma forte. Depois, houve a luta contra os pietistas e os pregadores autonomeados, especialmente os chamados "Irmãos" (*Gemeinschaftsbruder*), que eram tão santos aos seus próprios olhos que corriam o risco de voar para o céu em suas roupas de trabalho. Eles estavam puxando a rede de Cristo com toda a sua força, mas infelizmente na direção errada. A maioria deles se tornou Batista, e mais tarde pensadores livres. Houve brigas o tempo todo com aqueles que, mais cedo ou mais tarde, se revelavam como francamente incrédulos. Esses eram a maioria em muitas das "congregações" menores e, em alguns casos, a minoria luterana perdeu a propriedade da sua igreja. Em outros, a propriedade teve de ser vendida e o valor da venda dividido. Nesses casos, a regra era culpar o pastor por ter causado as dissensões. Essa culpa facilmente recaía nas suas costas. No entanto, era contra a palavra de Deus que eles estavam lutando, e foi Deus quem deu a vitória à sua palavra em todos os casos, embora nem sempre da mesma maneira. Seu poder era sempre manifestado muito claramente para que o pastor ou qualquer um dos membros pudesse reivindicar qualquer crédito. E ele não apenas fazia com que as tempestades cessassem e a luz do sol retornasse nos momentos certos, mas também fez os seus verdadeiros luteranos, um número pequeno, mas não desprezível, ver que não havia outro caminho para a paz do que pela luta.

Que a vida pessoal do pastor nem sempre é um caminho de rosas, não preciso dizer. No entanto, quero mencionar alguns detalhes, não para me colocar num pedestal, mas para justificar o título, "Abrindo fronteiras". Em primeiro lugar, não será errado mencionar as implicações para a saúde mental quando se fala de abrir fronteiras. Temo que o leitor não consiga imaginar o que isso significa para um homem cuja mente e alma foram educadas para apreciar tudo o que é bom, nobre e cheio de conteúdo intelectual; formadas pelo que para ele sempre será descrito como um lar excepcional, por um bom professor e pastor, por quase uma vintena de professores que eram em sua maioria homens excelentes; treinadas em todas as coisas boas por mais de vinte anos—você mal pode imaginar o que significa para uma pessoa assim ser subitamente largada na selva do sul do Brasil, em meio a pessoas cujas qualidades marcantes são analfabetismo, embriaguez, superficialidade e a mais grosseira das grosserias de linguagem e modos. Antes de receber o meu chamado para o Brasil, passei quase um ano entre os vagabundos, trabalhadores temporários e gente rude do nosso próprio oeste selvagem. O leitor terá que me perdoar por não explicar aqui como fui

cantados nessas campanhas eram caracterizados por um foco na conversão emocional, melodias simples e fáceis de cantar, e pela participação da congregação.

parar em tal companhia. Agora sei o que não sabia na época, que foi uma das escolas de Deus para o meu trabalho no Brasil. Mas quero apenas dizer que esses vagabundos não se comparam a alguns dos meus russos alemães no que diz respeito à grosseria da sua linguagem. Algumas vezes me senti agradecido por não ter tido a sorte de levar uma garota americana para esse ambiente, embora isso não signifique que uma verdadeira garota americana, se fosse colocada em uma atmosfera como essa pela vontade de Deus, não poderia ter sido perfeitamente feliz a seu serviço lá. E para que não me esqueça do lado positivo, quero lembrar a mim mesmo e ao leitor que esse triste desperdício em termos de analfabetismo e grosseria teve um oásis agradável para mim na pessoa do Mertens, que na verdade foi realmente a minha única "companhia" durante meu primeiro e segundo ano.

Já mostrei alguns exemplos que ilustram as implicações das muitas viagens cruéis a que o missionário é submetido em seu trabalho. Gostaria de voltar ao assunto mais uma vez com toda a seriedade, sem tirar nada da aspereza ao contar a história mostrando um lado humorístico. Eu nunca senti essas longas e cruéis viagens como um sacrifício pessoal da minha parte, mas como um desperdício inconcebível de forças que pertencem a Deus. As habilidades do missionário para o cumprimento eficiente dos seus múltiplos deveres, suas forças físicas, sua força nervosa, seu frescor mental, ficam todos tão indesculpavelmente reduzidos pelo fato de ele ficar demasiado tempo na sela, hora após hora. Uma vez, em um momento de fraqueza durante um desses passeios, contei os passos da minha mula durante um minuto e multipliquei esse número pelo número de minutos em dez horas, uma viagem que eu tinha que fazer com bastante frequência: um total de cerca de noventa mil solavancos. Seria loucura acreditar que um ser humano poderia pregar tão poderosamente, ou instruir tão bem, ou estar tão desperto para oportunidades de trabalho pastoral com indivíduos, depois de tantos solavancos para cima e para baixo, como ele o faria se os solavancos da estrada tivessem sido, em sua maior parte, absorvidos por um conjunto de boas molas de uma charrete. É a isso que se resume no fim: muito das forças dos missionários desperdiçadas, espalhadas pela estrada, por falta de um conjunto de molas de charrete debaixo dele. E não podemos comprar charretes no Brasil, e o missionário não pode importá-los como individuo, e o departamento de missão não tem dinheiro para enviá-los, ou sempre tem algum outro problema em algum lugar. O missionário não sabe onde realmente está a solução. Mas o seu coração sofre, não porque sua querida e velha carcaça esteja sofrendo, mas porque a obra do Senhor não está sendo feita como deveria.

Se me perdoarem por escrever mais algumas palavras sobre um assunto um tanto doloroso, gostaria de chamar a atenção para a parte mais cruel de uma viagem tão atroz. Trata-se da volta para casa em escuridão total, sob uma chuva torrencial em estradas onde cada passo pode trazer a morte. Não me refiro à morte por animais selvagens. Nunca encontrei um animal perigoso, nem fui atacado por ladrões. Refiro-me aos perigos de fraturar o crânio ou quebrar o pescoço em um galho pendurado, o perigo de cortar a garganta numa cana quebrada, o perigo de escorregar, cair e ser arrastado até a morte pelo próprio animal que está montando. Não estou inventando fantasias. Fui muitas vezes milagrosamente salvo de todos esses e outros perigos. Não estou buscando simpatia. Tenho sido tão feliz em meu trabalho a cada dia desses oito anos que não saberia o que fazer como manifestações de simpatia. Eu só quero completar o que comecei ao contar que esses passeios no escuro por horas a fio com perigosas incertezas pairando sobre a sua cabeça são a parte mais cruel da nossa vida na sela, e uma hora na sela nessas circunstâncias sempre me deixou mais nervoso do que cinco horas à luz do dia, ou sem chuva, ou em estradas boas e leves. Por isso quero salientar que nos casos em que a estrada é larga o suficiente para uma carroça, uma charrete com uma lanterna acoplada acabaria com a maior parte dessa pressão sobre os nervos.

Minha vida doméstica também continha suficiente "asperezas" para evitar que se tornasse monótona e insípida. Em um parágrafo anterior, eu me referi à nossa maneira de viver no antigo moinho. Mais tarde, na casa paroquial, tive com mais frequência a sensação de estar na minha própria casa, mas nem sempre me senti muito bem: Tive de conviver por anos com empregados homens de vários tipos, que também cozinhavam de forma bastante variada. Um deles era vidrado em sopas, fazia um excelente requeijão, e acreditava firmemente que a minha vaca estava enfeitiçada. Além disso, tinha o hábito de secar as suas meias encima da lata de café. Mais tarde, tive um cozinheiro que realmente sabia cozinhar, mas ele tinha outros defeitos, como, por exemplo, se servir do conteúdo da minha gaveta de dinheiro, o que não foi um grande prejuízo, pois a gaveta de dinheiro de um missionário está quase sempre vazia.

A casa pastoral foi bem pensada pelos representantes do Sínodo. Um prédio grande, de dois andares, com dezesseis cômodos, planejada para abrigar duas famílias de missionários, com o maior número de grandes janelas francesas que já vi em uma casa desse tamanho. Com exceção do meu escritório, as janelas não tinham vidro durante a guerra e por algum tempo depois. Não havia persianas. No Brasil, chove de vez em quando. Às vezes temos a sensação de que está sempre chovendo lá: E em cada chuva, a água escorria pelo teto na posição de barlavento da casa. Em algumas chuvas, todos os quatro lados pareciam estar posicionados no barlavento, pois a tempestade levava os lençóis de chuva de ponta a ponta. Mas fomos treinados, como a tripulação de um navio, para guardar todos os bens móveis no lado mais seco da casa. E quando o vento mudava, nós mudávamos tudo para o outro lado. Ouve situações em que estávamos sentados no sota-vento da casa e não percebíamos a chuva chegando pelo barlavento. Consequência? Deparava-nos com livros estragados ou com uma cama completamente molhada, ou até coberta com uma camada de argamassa soprada da parede inacabada. Isso também afetava os nossos nervos. Mas posso dizer que sempre tentava encontrar o lado engraçado das coisas. Um dos lados engraçados era o fato de que o chão era absolutamente à prova d'água. Nós tínhamos que fazer buracos nele para escoar a água. Mas depois de casado, e antes de ter a ideia dos buracos no assoalho, e sempre que mudávamos tudo para o lado seco, antes que o vento mudasse de lado, nós juntávamos as nossas mãos e dançávamos descalços no assoalho inundado do quarto de estudo e da sala de jantar. Esse era o lado engraçado, mas às vezes eu duvidava que a maioria das mulheres achasse isso engraçado. Mas, no final das contas, eu tinha um lar, e ele sempre foi um verdadeiro lar para mim. E depois de oito anos de construção, a casa estava quase pronta, e raramente chovia nos quartos ou molhava as camas.

Já antecipei a notícia de que, depois de alguns anos de vida de solteiro, encontrei uma mãe para o lar. Naqueles quatro anos de solidão, às vezes me perguntava como uma mulher me encontraria no sertão brasileiro para se casar comigo. Essas preocupações, como todas as preocupações, foram totalmente desnecessárias. No momento certo, e sem nenhuma ajuda da minha parte, Deus fez com que a jovem mais querida do mundo inteiro (para mim) se tornasse vizinha da casa paroquial. Naturalmente, o inevitável não demorou para acontecer. Quando noivamos, apareceram várias delegações de membro da congregação exigindo que o noivado fosse desfeito novamente, pois eles não iriam aceitar que uma jovem da congregação se tornasse a esposa do pastor deles. E apareceram delegações de não membros exigindo que eu não quebrasse o noivado pois criariam um escândalo nos jornais se eu o fizesse. Nenhuma das delegações alteram em nada o curso da história.

Nenhum de nós dois tinha dinheiro para um grande casamento. Na noite do nosso casamento civil, celebramos apenas um com o outro. Cinco dias depois, viajamos juntos para Ijuí, onde nos casamos na igreja, no que chamamos de nosso dia oficial de casamento. E um casamento simples, mas inesquecivelmente lindo foi preparado para nós pelo pastor Muller e a sua esposa, e pelo professor Naumann e sua esposa. Entre os convidados estavam vários pastores e professores a caminho de uma conferência. Fomos persuadidos a viajar com eles para a conferência. Em nosso retorno, pegamos emprestada a charrete do pastor Muller para os últimos 160 quilômetros. Estando no Brasil, não foi uma grande surpresa que o nosso eixo dianteiro tenha entortado ao cruzar o primeiro rio. A próxima coisa foi que minhas mulas caminharam até o centro de uma grande lagoa, aí pararam e olharam para mim como dizendo: "Venha e nos tire daqui se quiser". Foi o que eu fiz. Em seguida, atolamos até os eixos em uma lama pesada em um dos rios. As mulas puxaram como se houvessem sessenta delas, e as duas barras conectoras quebraram como palitos de dente. Acho que as mulas fizeram isso de propósito. De qualquer forma, fomos obrigados a descer e com lama até os nossos joelhos levantar o vagão. Na sequência, uma daquelas chuvas brasileiras de verdade começou a cair, e continuou até chegarmos em casa. Essa foi nossa viagem de lua de mel. Temos sido muito felizes desde então.

Se tivesse espaço, gostaria de escrever uma ou duas coisas sobre essa mulher maravilhosa que é minha esposa. As coisas mais importantes, no entanto, podem ser encontradas escritas no último capítulo do livro de Provérbios. Devo acrescentar que ela é russa alemã de nascimento, brasileira por adoção desde os seus onze anos de idade, americana por simpatia e casamento. Considerando que não frequentou escola, ela é uma excelente leitora. Em seus dias de confirmação e depois, ela memorizou todo o catecismo sinodal, inclusive a maior parte da introdução de Lutero. Quando ainda menina, ela percorreu 22 quilômetros a pé ida e volta no mesmo dia, na chuva e descalça, é claro, para ouvir um dos nossos concertos de coral. Como mãe, ela é uma das mais atualizadas educadora cientista que conheço. Sei que serei perdoado por revelar tanto da história da família, pois mulheres boas e interessadas já me perguntaram: "Você tem uma boa esposa?"

Fizeram-nos outras perguntas, uma ou duas das quais responderei aqui. "Vocês não usam aliança de casamento no Brasil?" Sim, usamos. Pelo menos as pessoas que têm dinheiro. Na época, nós não tínhamos. Mais tarde decidimos que docemente nos vingaríamos dessa situação comprando nossas alianças nada menos do que na Tiffany's em Nova Iorque. Foi o que fizemos. São alianças comum de ouro e nelas está gravado: "Urwahnfried—1918". Nada mais, mas aqui há muito conteúdo. Urwahnfried é uma palavra composta de raízes de palavras alemãs antigas e significa, no português moderno, "realização". Ou, de forma mais explícita, "O Lugar onde minha Luta pelos Ideais mais elevados e de maior alcance na Vida alcançam Plenitude na Paz da Vitória." Urwahnfried é o nome da casa pastoral em Guarani. É também o nome de nossa estação de correio particular, que é muito importante, pois antigamente grande parte da nossa correspondência ia para uma cidadezinha na fronteira com a República Oriental do Uruguai, chamada Quaraí. Desde que a batizamos com esse nome, não sei de nenhum caso de correspondência extraviada.

Fomos perguntados sobre a existência de médicos, parteiras e enfermeiras no Brasil. Acho que o pequeno Siegfried pode ajudar-nos a responder essas perguntas, a pequena criança ensolarada da floresta com os olhos dançantes, que não sabe que extremamente infeliz é por ter nascido na floresta primitiva sem um médico ou uma enfermeira. O nosso médico mais próximo estava a mais de 90 quilômetros de distância, o que significa 30 a 60 horas de ida e volta, dependendo do clima. Devemos dar crédito a esse homem por não ter nos causado nenhum problema ou preocupação em todos esses anos, pois quando precisávamos dele, não conseguíamos chegar até ele. E quando conseguíamos chegar, já não precisávamos mais dele. E se ele tivesse que vir até nós, teria nos custado mais ou menos um mês de salário. Sobre parteiras, havia muitas dentro do nosso pequeno círculo em Guarani, mas apenas uma delas tinha um pouco de treinamento ou leitura. Algumas das demais traziam consigo a noite inteira da ignorância e superstição medievais. Só para mencionar um caso, suficiente para causar arrepios nos americanos: Uma das mais populares deitava os bebês recém-nascidos no chão, praticamente sem agasalho, por cerca de uma hora, para que os espíritos malignos pudessem evaporar. Preferimos, por razões que nos parecem válidas, receber o pequeno Siegfried sozinhos. Em todos os aspectos essenciais, ele recebeu a mesma recepção que teria recebido em um bom hospital, e Deus fez o resto. Seríamos desonestos se disséssemos que queríamos que tivesse sido diferente.

Quanto à minha saúde, tive uma hemorragia de estômago no começo de 1916, em consequência daquelas longas e cruéis viagens a cavalo. De passagem, menciono que em um momento de grande fraqueza, sentindo que poderia desmaiar em qualquer momento, fui obrigado a me levantar e realizar uma cerimônia de casamento. Apesar disso e de outras coisas, fiquei bom. Mas em 1922 tive quatro recaídas, mais ou menos a uma distância de 8 a 10 horas de casa, e sem nenhum outro jeito de chegar em casa a não ser a cavalo (não havia outra opção melhor). Cada uma daquelas crises me levou às portas da morte e me manteve em uma condição de extrema fraqueza por um mês ou mais. Quando recebi permissão para tirar uma licença de um ano, eu já tinha tido um ataque e, quando o médico me deu a permissão, eu estava muito fraco. Quando recebi a permissão para tirar um ano de licença, eu já tinha tido uns dois ataques e quando o dinheiro chegou, depois de oito ou nove meses, as outras três já estavam no passado. Fui para um bom hospital na Alemanha e depois de uma semana de exames minuciosos, fiquei agradavelmente surpreso ao saber que não havia absolutamente nenhum traço de defeito em meu estômago. Como não havia dúvida alguma sobre a veracidade das hemorragias, os médicos do hospital pareciam incapazes de explicar o caso com uma das suas teorias. Para mim, a explicação é simples, pois eu acredito em milagres: Os médicos teriam gostado muito de ter me submetido a uma cirurgia como prevenção para evitar uma possível crise futura. Educadamente recusei.

Ao concluir essa breve narrativa descrevendo oito anos de trabalho duro para Cristo nas selvas do Brasil, sinto que não devo omitir uma palavra de Cristo que todo missionário conhece, acredita e valoriza. Está registrada em Marcos 10.29–30: "Em verdade lhes digo que não há ninguém que tenha deixado casa, irmãos, irmãs, mãe, pai, filhos ou campos por minha causa e por causa do evangelho, que não receba, já no presente, cem vezes mais casas, irmãos, irmãs, mães, filhos e campos, com perseguições; e, no mundo por vir, receberá a vida eterna." É difícil expressar o quanto me senti revigorado pelo retorno ao pleno gozo das múltiplas bênçãos da civilização durante minha estada na Alemanha e nos Estados Unidos, nem o quanto sou grato por toda a bondade demonstrada pelos irmãos de ambos os lados do Atlântico. Mas não existe lugar igual a Urwahnfried, e não há substituto para a bênção especial de Deus no campo missionário. O desejo do meu coração e a minha oração diária é estar de volta ao trabalho logo depois destas páginas terem sido impressas, lá onde já escolhi o meu local de sepultamento. A única coisa que é mais satisfatória e abençoada do que trabalhar duro para Cristo é mais trabalho duro para Cristo.

Albert Ernst Heinrich Lehenbauer

Abriendo fronteras para Cristo en las selvas de Brasil

[Jesús dijo:] "Serán mis testigos . . . hasta lo último de la tierra." (Hechos 1:8)

Traducido por
LUZ M. KRAMER

Editado por
ROBERTO ALEJANDRO WEBER

La Serie de Monografías del Instituto Histórico Concordia tiene como objetivo publicar y difundir investigaciones relevantes y valiosas relacionadas con la historia de la Iglesia Luterana confesional en Norteamérica, especialmente aquellas que utilizan el material custodiado por el archivo y la biblioteca del Instituto Histórico Concordia, así como el material de los archivos y bibliotecas de otras entidades de la Iglesia Luterana—Sínodo de Misuri.

Daniel N. Harmelink, Editor de la Serie

John C. Wohlrabe Jr., Lawrence R. Rast Jr., John W. Sias, Editores Asociados

Volúmenes Anteriores

Seminex in Print: A Comprehensive Bibliography of Published Material and Selected Archival Resources for Historical Research. Compilado por David O. Berger junto con Daniel N. Harmelink (2021).

The Emigration of the Saxon Lutherans in the Year 1838 and Their Settlement in Perry County, Missouri por J. F. Koestering. Traducido por Brian Lutz y G. H. Naumann. Revisado para publicación por Matthew Carver (2022).

Rediscovering the Issues Surrounding the 1974 Concordia Seminary Walkout. Editado por Ken Schurb (2023).

A Hundredfold Harvest: A Survey of Mission Work in Travancore, South India, in the Early 1900s. Heinrich Nau. Traducido por Matthew Carver (2025)..

Publicado por Concordia Publishing House
3558 S. Jefferson Ave., St. Louis, MO 63118-3968
1-800-325-3040 • cph.org

Publicado originalmente como «Roughing It for Christ in the Wilds of Brazil», Zwickau: Johannes Herrmann, 1923.

Las citas bíblicas corresponden a la versión Reina-Valera 1960 o la versión autorizada de la Biblia.

Todas las fotografías de este libro se publican con la autorización de la familia Lehenbauer.

Impreso en los Estados Unidos de América.

Albert Ernst Heinrich Lehenbauer

(13 de febrero de 1891—29 de abril de 1955)

El Rev. Albert E. H. Lehenbauer nació en West Ely, Missouri, el 13 de febrero de 1891, el octavo de los nueve hijos de Conrad y Catherine (Preusser) Lehenbauer. Su padre murió cuando él tenía cinco años y, desde entonces, su madre se aseguró de que, luego de su confirmación un Domingo de Ramos (en 1905 por el pastor Pflanz), continuara su educación y comenzara sus estudios en el Seminario Concordia de Saint Louis. Se graduó en 1913. Albert deseaba profundamente ingresar al campo misionero extranjero y servir como misionero en China. Sin embargo, antes de dejar su tierra natal por el Oriente, decidió esperar un año. Con el inicio de la Primera Guerra Mundial en 1917, ya no fue posible enviar misioneros a China. Esto llevó a Albert a aceptar un llamado a Brasil, donde dos de sus hermanos, Conrad (quien sirvió como pastor en Arroio do Meio) y George (quien sirvió como pastor en Santa Cruz), habían sido enviados previamente.

Albert Lehenbauer llegó a Porto Alegre en 1915, en el Día de los Navegantes (un día festivo en Porto Alegre que se celebra cada 2 de febrero). Puesto que no hablaba portugués y todo los comercios estaban cerrados, después de varios intentos, fue capaz de localizar el seminario luterano. Después de visitar brevemente a sus dos hermanos, Albert viajó por tren a Ijuí, donde el Pastor E. Miller esperaba su llegada. Desde allí, viajaron en caballo y carreta a Linha 23 y después a Guarany, su nuevo lugar de residencia. Su primer sermón, en abril de ese mismo año, se basó en San Lucas 18:9-14, un texto que describe muy claramente la gracia y el amor de Dios. Sobre esta misma gracia y amor de Dios, Albert predicó, enseñó, y escribió durante todos sus años de ministerio, siendo un gran ejemplo para sus feligreses localizados en 13 estaciones misioneras, incluyendo su hogar en Linha 15, al cual afectuosamente llamaba *Urwahnfried* (cumplimiento). Precisamente por esta razón comenzó a organizar reuniones con jóvenes que consideraba buenos candidatos para el ministerio pastoral, enseñándoles la doctrina cristiana los domingos por la noche, siempre que le era posible.

Puesto que creía en la importancia de buenos materiales de lectura para la educación cristiana, fue el primer editor del directorio anual titulado *Luther-Kalender*. También escribió un gran número de artículos para el *Kirchenblatt*, el "Leitor Brasileiro", y otras publicaciones dentro y fuera de Brasil. Su estilo claro y sencillo al escribir reflejaba su fe en las enseñanzas de la Biblia y en los escritos de Martín Lutero.

Debido a sus muchos y variados dones dados por Dios, pronto fue elegido para ser un miembro del Comité de Misiones y poco después para ser el director del Departamento de Misión de todo el Brasil. Además, sirvió como vice-presidente del cuerpo eclesiástico luterano de Brasil del "Libro de Concordia" entre 1928 y 1932. Sus responsabilidades requirieron de muchos viajes, no sólo en el estado de Rio Grande do Sul, sino también en el extranjero.

El 31 de diciembre de 1918, Albert Lehenbauer se casó con Helena Priebe. Seis de sus ocho hijos nacieron en Brasil, en *Urwahnfried*. Su segundo hijo, Reginald, nació en Hannibal, Missouri, en 1923, mientras la familia disfrutaba su año sabático en los Estados Unidos. Al final de su año sabático, Albert y Helena y sus dos hijos regresaron a Brasil y llegaron a *Urwahnfried* el 12 de Noviembre de 1923. El hijo menor nació en Argentina en 1939.

Albert había notado anteriormente que, en ciertos lugares donde los miembros de su iglesia habían sembrado distintos granos, cada año que pasaba la tierra agotada producía menos y menos. Entonces comenzó a investigar este problema con la esperanza de encontrar una solución. Como lector entusiasta que era, Albert descubrió eventualmente un artículo que explicaba cómo ciertas plantas (legumbres) incorporaban nitrógeno a la tierra, un fertilizante natural. Y aún mejor, estas plantas crecían donde otras plantas ya no podían hacerlo. Al enterarse de que la soja es una de esas plantas que producen nitrógeno, quedó convencido de que cultivarla sería una buena solución para el problema que enfrentaban los miembros de su iglesia. Siendo así, al regresar de su año sabático trajo a Brasil una botella con un puñado de semillas de soja del campo de sus padres en Missouri. Una vez en *Urwahnfried*, Albert sembró las semillas en su jardín. En 1924, cuando cosechó lo que las primeras semillas produjeron, guardó la mitad de las semillas y distribuyó el resto en pequeñas cajas de fósforos que contenían dos o tres semillas para cada parroquiano con estas instrucciones: "Siémbrenlas y, cuando produzcan el próximo año, den la mitad a su vecino o amigo y díganles que hagan lo mismo con su primera cosecha". Albert también siguió estas directrices y continuó la distribución de semillas después de las cosechas subsecuentes.

Después de algunas cosechas, las semillas de soja comenzaron a multiplicarse hasta tal punto que algunas personas reportaron que una sola planta podía producir 400 vainas. Más adelante, en un artículo que escribió, Albert urgía a los agricultores a plantar soja debido al gran rendimiento y a sus variados usos culinarios.

Los agricultores que sembraron soja descubrieron que, en poco tiempo, tenían gran cantidad de semillas, pero poca o ninguna idea de qué hacer con ellas. Primero intentaron tostarlas y molerlas y luego preparar una bebida similar al café, pero la soja obstruía sus molinillos de café, y al verter agua caliente sobre el polvo de soja, se formaba una capa densa de aceite que hacía que la bebida caliente fuera imbebible.

Otros intentaron usar el polvo de soja para hacer pan, el cual no estaba tan mal cuando era recién sacado del horno. Sin embargo, al cabo de algunas horas, el pan exudaba aceite y se volvía poco apetecible. Por lo tanto, se abandonaron los intentos para hacer pan de soja.

Finalmente, sin saber qué hacer con la soja y sin querer cuestionar las buenas intenciones del pastor, uno de los agricultores decidió darla a sus cerdos. En poco tiempo, esto causó una auténtica revolución en la industria porcina del estado. Los cerdos no solo crecían más rápido, sino que también engordaban más. Lo mismo ocurrió cuando los granjeros alimentaron con soja a sus vacas, utilizadas para la producción de leche y carne. Eventualmente, la soja comenzó a ser utilizada para elaborar aceite de cocina y lo que quedaba de este proceso se convirtió en el principal alimento para cerdos y vacas. De ahí en adelante, el cultivo y la cosecha de la soja fue un éxito garantizado.

En la actualidad, Brasil es el segundo productor más grande de soja y Argentina es el tercero. La producción y exportación de soja de Brasil continúa creciendo rápidamente. Sin duda, esta humilde semilla cambió las vidas de los agricultores de *Urwahnfried* en el estado de Rio Grande do Sul, y de agricultores en otros estados de Brasil, como también de Argentina y Paraguay. Hoy, la soja es utilizada en una gran variedad de productos comestibles y no comestibles.

En los primeros meses de 1937, después de servir como pastor y misionero en Brasil por 22 años, el Pastor Albert Lehenbauer aceptó un llamado a la Argentina para ser el director de una escuela pre-teológica (Colegio Concordia). En ese entonces, Argentina no tenía un seminario. Esto significaba que los seminaristas de Argentina tenían que trasladarse al seminario luterano de Brasil o a los Estados Unidos. Sin embargo, la iglesia estaba muy interesada en llamar a alguien que trabaje en una escuela preparatoria para formar a los futuros pastores en el idioma español. La idea era formar pastores que pudieran hablar español para que sirvieran en la iglesia argentina (y después en otras naciones hispano-hablantes de Sudamérica). Esta escuela se fundó en Villa Crespo [Entre Ríos] y Albert sirvió como su director desde 1937 a 1942. En 1942, cuando viajó a los Estados Unidos, el Pastor Lehenbauer convenció al Departamento de Misión de la Iglesia Luterana del Sínodo de Missouri sobre la necesidad de ayudar a construir un seminario en Argentina. Albert fue el primer director después de que se construyera el Seminario Concordia en Villa Ballester, en las afueras de Buenos Aires. Ocupó este cargo desde 1942 hasta 1946, cuando pasó a desempeñarse como profesor de teología en dicho seminario.

Durante sus años de trabajo pastoral en Argentina, el Pastor Albert fue también co-editor del *Kirchengebote* (1938–40), editor del *Evangelical Lutheran Hymnal* (que también contenía algunos himnos traducidos por él al español). Además, encontró tiempo para ser co-editor de numerosos libros editados en portugués y en español durante este período, y escribió numerosos artículos presentados en convenciones nacionales en las Iglesias de Argentina y Brasil.

En 1955, durante el jubileo de los 50 años de la Iglesia Evangélica Luterana Argentina en Aldea San Juan (Entre Ríos), Albert Lehenbauer estuvo encargado de cerrar la actividad con un devocional. Se suponía que esta era su última participación oficial en la iglesia antes de su retiro. Poco después de abordar el tren de regreso a Buenos Aires, comenzó a sufrir un severo dolor de cabeza. Sus dos hermanos, George y Conrad, y sus dos yernos, el Pastor Fernando Höhn y el Pastor Edgar Kroger, viajaban con él, al igual que otros pastores y líderes de la iglesia que se dirigían a Buenos Aires. Aunque sus yernos quisieron llevarlo al hospital inmediatamente, Albert pensó que era mejor ir directamente a Buenos Aires, creyendo que pronto se pondría mejor. Puesto que su dolor de cabeza empeoraba, pidió su Biblia y leyó las palabras del Salmo 23 y el versículo del Salmo 119:105. Poco después de esto, ya no pudo hablar más de manera coherente. El Pastor R. Hasse se unió a los hombres que ministraron a Albert en ese momento y le preguntó si tenía fe en Jesucristo. Puesto que no era capaz de responder con palabras, Albert no dudó en hacer un gesto afirmativo con su cabeza. A pesar de que intentó comunicarse varias veces más, nadie logró entenderlo. Después de un corto tiempo, pasó a un estado inconsciente y murió de un derrame cerebral en el hospital de Buenos Aires tres días después, el 29 de Abril de 1955.

El funeral de Albert se llevó a cabo en el Seminario Concordia en José León Suarez, partido de San Martín (Buenos Aires), Argentina. Se predicaron tres sermones diferentes durante el servicio: El Presidente, Rev. F. Lange, predicó en español; el Rev. S. H. Beckmann predicó en alemán; y el Rev. Dr. F. Hasse predicó en portugués, mientras que el Rev. Ern Hoapp ofició la sepultura. El Pastor Albert Lehenbauer fue sepultado en el cementerio de San Martín.

Después de la muerte de Albert, Helena Lehenbauer continuó viviendo por algunos años en su pequeña casa en Misiones, Argentina. En Octubre de 1970 se mudó a la ciudad de Nueva York (EEUU), para vivir con su hija menor Mónica, hasta su muerte, el 17 de Febrero de 1986. Helena fue sepultada junto a su hijo Reginald en Fayetteville, Carolina del Norte (EEUU). Su nieto, el Rev. Walter Lehenbauer ofició su sepelio.

Rev. Walter Lehenbauer
Cloquet, Minnesota, EUA

Introducción histórica

El Rev. Albert Ernst Heinrich Lehenbauer nació el 13 de febrero de 1891 en West Ely, Missouri (EE.UU.). Fue enviado por la LCMS como misionero a Brasil en 1914. Se estableció en Santa Rosa (actual Ubiretama), donde se casó con Helena Priebe y tuvo ocho hijos. Junto con los líderes locales, fundó la Unión Colonial de Linha 23 de *Julho*, donde fomentó el cultivo de soja y otras prácticas agrícolas en reuniones con los líderes, así como el estudio de la Palabra.

Y este pastor Albert Lehenbauer fue un instrumento de Dios, no sólo para mantener la fe de estos inmigrantes luteranos que necesitaban asistencia espiritual, sino también para mejorar la vida de los agricultores que vivían con grandes dificultades y con pocas escuelas, pocos recursos técnicos para trabajar en el área agrícola.

Así que decidió traer un puñado de semillas de soya de Estados Unidos en uno de sus viajes de vacaciones, que distribuyó entre los colonos que participaban en sus estudios bíblicos.

Con ello, no sólo encontró una forma alternativa de la mera supervivencia para la sociedad que le rodeaba, sino también soluciones, estableciendo una revolución agrícola. A partir de 1924 se convirtió en el agente de transformación más importante de la historia de la ciudad. Además de su fiel labor como misionero, pastor y educador de la LCMS, también utilizó sus otras cualificaciones en educación y agricultura para servir a sus congregantes.

A través de su trabajo en la sociedad, se convirtió en protagonista en beneficio del bienestar social de la sociedad en la que se encontraba. No era un mero espectador. El pastor Albert fue un líder de la transformación, inspirando nuevos proyectos, fortaleciendo alianzas y fomentando una agricultura diferenciada en todo el país. A través de sus acciones, fue un instrumento de cambio que ha repercutido en esa sociedad hasta el día de hoy.

En noviembre de 2024, cuando se celebró el centenario de la soja en Brasil en la Fenasoja (Feria Nacional de la Soja) en Santa Rosa, este pastor fue el protagonista de esta hermosa historia de misión y transformación.

El Pastor Lehenbauer trabajó aquí en Brasil durante 23 años. Luego aceptó un llamado a Argentina, ¡donde continuó su misión!

Rev Mario Lehenbauer—Pastor Emérito
Iglesia Evangélica Luterana de Brasil

ABRIENDO FRONTERAS PARA CRISTO EN LAS SELVAS DE BRASIL

HABÍAN PASADO CERCA DE OCHO AÑOS CUANDO el Reverendo C. Trünow y yo nos embarcamos desde New York en el *S. S. Vasari* con rumbo a nuestros respectivos campos misioneros en América del Sur. Él iba para Argentina, yo tenía un llamado en Brasil. El viaje en el océano hacia Rio de Janeiro, donde nosotros tomaríamos rumbos diferentes, fue suave y soleado. Pero después comenzaron las dificultades. En la oficina de aduana me di cuenta de que me faltaba la mitad del dinero para pagar mi impuesto. Afortunadamente, el señor Trünow me prestó la cantidad que necesitaba.

En el Puerto de Santos, conocido por su exportación de café, casi me dejan debido al hecho de que la hora de salida de mi embarcación a vapor de línea costera había sido avanzada en mi ausencia, sin mi conocimiento. Gasté mi último dinero en efectivo contratando un bote a remo. Pero tuve éxito alcanzando la embarcación a vapor. Esta acción del capitán, la cual consideré un gran acto de rudeza en contra de mi valiosa persona, hizo que me sea imposible, por la falta de fondos, comprar algún refresco durante los cuatro días restantes de viaje. ¡Ah, las fantásticas naranjas, bananas, cocos y piñas que no pude comprar! Pero eso no fue ninguna mala suerte comparado con lo que hubiera sido si yo no hubiera alcanzado la embarcación a vapor.

No hubiera habido oportunidad de escribir ni tampoco de girar dinero en la fecha de mi llegada a la comunidad hermana del sur de Brasil y yo sabía que nadie me hubiera esperado en el muelle. Desembarcamos en Porto Alegre, la capital de Rio Grande do Sul, que es el estado más al sur de la República de Brasil, en un día de fiesta y encontré cerrados la mayoría de los negocios. Nuestro seminario estaba ubicado en ese momento en un suburbio desapercibido, y me fue difícil conseguir cualquier información sobre su ubicación. Tres veces y desde tres ubicaciones totalmente diferentes, me dieron direcciones para llegar al mismo seminario católico. Al medio día, almorcé las uvas más deliciosas, las cuales compré con mis últimas monedas (conservando algunas para el pago del transporte) y utilizando el lenguaje de las señas; puesto que no tenía la menor idea de que en portugués, el lenguaje de este país, esta fruta tiene el mismo nombre que en el latín "uva". Tampoco sabía si las estaba comprando por libra, pie o ramo. Al final, después de arrastrar mi equipaje por todas partes durante cinco horas, me encontré a un alemán quien había escuchado alguna vez a uno de nuestros profesores predicar y pudo indicarme el camino a nuestro seminario.

Después de unos pocos días agradables entre los hermanos de la fe de Porto Alegre, visité brevemente a cada uno de mis dos hermanos, quienes habían comenzado la obra misionera en Brasil un año antes que yo. Después, abordé el tren del ferrocarril brasilero, con rumbo a mi propio campo misionero. Su nombre es Guarany y por una omisión inconcebible de quienes hacen los mapas, no se le puede encontrar en la mayoría de los mapas. Por mi parte, preferiría que se hubiese omitido el Polo Norte en todos los atlas, pues es un lugar que no tiene ningún uso para nadie, mientras que Guarany es, para algunas personas, incluyéndome a mí mismo, el centro de la tierra.

Después de dos días de mareos en la estrecha, también curvilínea y tembleque línea ferroviaria, por fin llegué a Ijuhy, que en ese tiempo era la terminal de la vía, donde el reverendo Emil Müller me dio la bienvenida. Todavía había una distancia de 60 millas que me separaba de la terminal de mi esperanza y de mis expectativas, caminos rurales estrechos que debíamos conquistar en una carreta que yo había traído conmigo para el reverendo Müller. Como consecuencia de las lluvias torrenciales, el tiempo usual de 16 horas para esta distancia se alargó a tres días completos. El primer día fue a lo largo del camino casi terminado para la continuación del ferrocarril, al cual yo agregué el pronombre de primera persona singular y lo llamé "mi ferrocarril". En el segundo y tercer día, mi valor fue avivado por la seguridad del reverendo Müller, quien me animaba repetidamente diciendo: "Después, cuando ya hayamos conquistado esta colina ante nosotros, vamos a estar mucho más cerca de lo que estamos en este momento". Este mismo alivio me sirvió mucho en mi labor misionera más adelante, cuando el camino fue mucho más elevado y enlodado.

Finalmente subimos la última colina. Llegamos a Guarany. La "y" final en muchas palabras sudamericanas es una palabra indígena para "agua" o "río". Pero Guarany no es en el presente el nombre de un río, sino de una colonización grande llevada a cabo por el Estado Gubernamental de Rio Grande do Sul. De esta colonia grande, sólo me interesó un pequeño grupo, que fue establecido casi exclusivamente por ruso-alemanes. Traten de imaginarse un pedazo grande de un pastel de 15 millas de largo y 7 de ancho. La parte superior del pastel es puro bosque brasilero primitivo e intacto, que consistente en árboles con troncos torcidos y un matorral de enredadera densa, arbustos, bambú, helechos, etc. Ahora imagínense ustedes mismos cortando este pastel a lo largo en franjas de 1-1/5 millas de ancho. Mis disculpas por agobiar sus mentes con estas fracciones, pero ellas vienen del hecho de que el gobierno brasilero utiliza el sistema métrico de pesos y medidas. Me gustaría que los Estados Unidos también utilizaran este sistema. Donde sea que el cuchillo haya cortado el pastel, nosotros debemos imaginarnos caminos de herradura, en muchos lugares incluso cerrados desde arriba por densas ramas de árboles y las enredaderas que crecen en ellos. Con el pasar del tiempo, estos caminos de herradura se ampliaron en caminos de carretas y carros y algunos de los más importantes pudieron ser utilizados para el tráfico de carretas cuando yo llegué allí. Ahora, por favor, corte en la mitad del pastel, convirtiendo cada tira larga en dos más cortas. Este es nuestro único cruce de camino, y uno muy pobre, puesto que muchos de los tocones parecían haber escogido sus lugares en el camino y no a los lados, y la cuneta de drenaje corre exactamente por el centro del camino. En distintas partes del camino puedes encontrarte con un barrial a la vista y no estar seguro si debes caminar, nadar, saltar, o volar. Tan reciente como 1921 supe de un caso donde el caballo de un inmigrante desapareció repentina y completamente en tal barrial y apenas pudo ser salvado de ahogarse. Tu incertidumbre no es, sin embargo, la culpa del barrial, sino de la inexperiencia. Todavía eres un novato en asuntos de caminos brasileros, me decía. Vas a aprender pronto.

Ahora, vamos a partir cada una de las porciones del pastel en dos más angostas, lo cual no las hace un camino o senda, sino solamente una línea de inspección y después cortémoslas totalmente en pedazos de un poco más de media milla de largo y 280 yardas de ancho. Estos tramos que contienen cerca de 62 acres de tierra de bosque son los "lotes rurales" o granjas de los inmigrantes, vendidas a ellos en términos muy fáciles por el Estado Gubernamental a un precio de cerca de 125 dólares americanos. Además, los inmigrantes fueron transportados de sus hogares anteriores al nuevo lugar por el Gobierno Federal de Brasil, lo cual no fue un mal negocio para nada. La mayoría de las granjas tenían agua corriente ya fuera de una quebrada, de un manantial o de un río.

Cuando hablamos de ruso-alemanes, nos referimos a gente de extracción puramente alemana quienes, sin embargo, han sido habitantes de Rusia por una o más generaciones. En sus colonias alemanas en Rusia más o menos sin mezcla alguna, preservaron la mayoría de sus características físicas, mentales y culturales que habían traído de Alemania, una o más generaciones atrás. Por el idioma y por sus costumbres me siento forzado a recordar cosas que leí sobre la vida alemana de hace más de cien años atrás. Esto incluye algunas cualidades muy buenas y algunas malas. Algunos de ellos, no todos, adoptaron de sus contextos rusos y polacos la inclinación a mentir y a robar.

Casi todos ellos son carpinteros en el sentido más comprehensible del término y son capaces de producir una cantidad extraordinaria de variados artículos con tan solo los árboles del bosque y unas pocas herramientas simples a su servicio. Los he visto tallar puertas perfectamente derechas sin trazar una sola línea; también serruchar sus tablas a mano con una velocidad considerable y disfrutando de su trabajo; también hacer los más finos productos para pulir la madera con muy pocos aparatos y sin productos de barniz ya preparados. Si alguna vez alguien vino fácilmente a la tierra más apropiada para sus necesidades particulares, estos fueron los inmigrantes ruso-alemanes que vinieron a Brasil en los últimos diez años antes de la gran guerra. Me gustaría agregar que todos ellos estuvieron agradecidos por ello y por el clima subtropical sano y agradable, y por haber sido separados de los horrores de esa catástrofe mundial.

En este pastel de migas, establecido por cerca de mil familias inmigrantes, yo debía hacerme cargo de mi campo, para bien o para mal. Di por sentado que sería para bien y sentí gozo en pensar en la selva virgen y el suelo virgen en los asuntos en la iglesia y la escuela. Pero no pasó mucho tiempo para que me diera cuenta de que yo debería tener algunos marcos para cortar y algunas tablas para serruchar en mi trabajo misionero. Pero ¿por qué hablar de trabajo misionero en lo más mínimo? ¿Eran paganas estas personas?

De nombre, eran luteranos. Pero en la mayoría de los casos su luteranismo terminaba con el nombre y el bautismo y otros certificados que habían traído con ellos. La llamada Iglesia Luterana de Rusia sufrió, antes de la guerra, todas las enfermedades de las Iglesias estatales unidas de Alemania, y además tenía uno o dos males especiales propios. El peor mal no era que los pastores fueron forzados algunas veces a comulgar luteranos de la manera luterana y a los miembros de la iglesia reformada en su propia manera en el mismo altar. Lo peor fue que los pastores eran, primera y principalmente, oficiales del gobierno ruso, teniendo como tarea principal llevar los registros que servían como una base para el reclutamiento militar, y solo secundariamente eran pastores del rebaño de Cristo. También, en la mayoría de los casos, ellos estaban tan sobrecargados con las congregaciones que raramente podían visitarlas más de una o dos veces por año, aun así, conducían dos servicios cada día de la semana mientras hacían su circuito. Cuando ellos estaban presentes, los agobiaba tanto la rutina de trabajo que el trabajo principal del pastor, alimentar las almas inmortales con la predicación de la Palabra, podía recibir solo una mínima parte de su atención y de sus facultades físicas. Estaba totalmente fuera de discusión que ellos mismos instruyeran a sus cientos de catecúmenos. Muchos de estos últimos vieron a su pastor por primera vez en su vida en el día de su confirmación. Se dudaba mucho si en promedio el pastor conocía personalmente el 1% de sus feligreses, ya fuera en el día de la confirmación o después de morir.

El servicio dominical usual consistía en la lectura de un sermón por un, así llamado, maestro, quien también tomaba el lugar del pastor en la instrucción de los jóvenes y en gran parte del trabajo pastoral real en la mayoría de las congregaciones. La mayoría de estos maestros no tenían ninguna formación, eran incapaces de explicar las principales doctrinas de la fe cristiana, y usualmente estaban contentos con que sus catecúmenos memorizaran las partes principales del Catecismo de una manera que no fuera tan incorrecta. Lejos de escribir libros, los pastores no podían ni siquiera suministrar los libros luteranos que se importaban de Alemania o América. El suministro de libros fue dejado en manos de los judíos. Es verdad que había poco interés en los buenos libros. Pero, ¿no eran los pastores las personas que deberían haber creado ese interés, y no hubiera crecido tal interés si solo se hubieran suministrado esos libros? Algunos de nosotros, los hijos más jóvenes del Sínodo de Missouri, nunca nos dimos cuenta de lo que teníamos con el suministro espléndido de libros y revistas buenos e interesantes, y muchos de nosotros somos tan desagradecidos como los nueve leprosos, porque no los leemos como deberíamos.

Bajo estas condiciones en Rusia, muchos de estos niños ruso-alemanes, hijos de Dios por el bautismo, crecieron sin entender realmente las principales doctrinas de su fe, sin saber por qué ellos eran llamados luteranos. En verdad, hubo muchos sermones luteranos buenos que les fueron leídos en sus reuniones hogareñas (las cuales se llamaban "escuelas", pero que no siempre fueron utilizadas para propósitos escolares); pero les faltó la llave para entender estos sermones, difícilmente entendían el idioma y, por consiguiente, captaban muy poco o nada de ellos. Y así muchos de ellos crecieron dentro de la iglesia luterana visible, mantenidos en ella por costumbres y por cierta presión proveniente del estado, pero siendo paganos en sus corazones, sin creer que la Biblia es la Palabra de Dios y sin desear ser guiados por su instrucción. No es fácil para mí escribir esto. No fue fácil tampoco creerlo. Pero mi propósito actual no es tapar la realidad, sino decir la verdad al describir el fondo de mi labor. Me propuse mostrar el porqué nosotros hablamos de obra misionera entre los llamados luteranos. Y en el tiempo de mi llegada a Guarany, un número deplorable de estas mil familias habían demostrado la verdad de lo que he escrito. Cientos de familias decidieron asistir a la iglesia bautista, porque fueron fácilmente persuadidas de que su fe luterana era una fe sin obras y muerta. Otros cientos de familias, que habían sentido caer sobre ellas las ataduras del control estatal en el pasado, decidieron ahora desechar la influencia de las buenas costumbres por considerarlas igualmente opresivas y por demostrar ser en realidad cien por ciento paganas.

Y ahí estaba yo, deseando conocer a este tipo de personas interesantes, pero no siempre agradables. Antes de que yo llegara, sin embargo, Dios ya había construido una escuela especial con el propósito de ayudarme en los primeros pasos de mi futura labor. No había casa parroquial lista para mí y se me ofreció usar gratis una pequeña casa vacante como mi primer domicilio temporal. La casa era parte de un molino de agua y cuando yo llegué en mi carro al patio de la casa ubicada en un valle solitario, el molinero (quien sería más adelante mi maestro) estaba parado en la puerta de entrada. Su nombre era Mertens y era un hombre poco común. Me temo que, a pesar de su amistosa bienvenida, su primera apariencia no me dio el sentimiento animador y de gran alegría que ahora experimento con tan solo pensar en él. Su figura se doblaba y dos accidentes casi fatales lo habían condenado a ser llamado por todos los que le conocían "El viejo", aunque estaba en la plenitud de su vida. Pero pronto comencé a sentir la calidez que emanaba de esa alma grande y maravillosa. Él no tenía educación alguna. Fue felizmente inocente, como la mayoría de sus compatriotas, de todas las leyes y normas gramaticales. Pero él hablaba, leía y escribía cuatro idiomas, sin contar Yidis, en el cual era también un maestro. En ocasiones, palabras largas se cruzaban en su lengua, o con una sílaba entrecortada o invertida. Pero él no se preocupaba por la forma. Su memoria era un milagro para mí, y parecía que nunca había olvidado nada que hubiera visto, oído, o leído. Sus libros llenaban una repisa de 1.5 metros de alto, e incluían media docena de los volúmenes de la edición "Luther" de St. Louis. Algunas de las glorias que lo coronaban eran un sentido del humor espontáneo que nunca cesaba, piedad genuina sin pietismo, y una buena reputación con amigos y enemigos.

Dentro de su molino tenía lo que él mismo llamaba un correo misionero. Con un corazón tan lleno de fe no podía ser de otra manera. Él solamente aprovechaba una buena oportunidad. Y esto era porque a su molino venían los representantes de todas las tendencias religiosas para moler su maíz. Y mientras sus granos caían entre las piedras del molino, con frecuencia los pensamientos más profundos de todos estos corazones eran molidos entre las piedras de la mente poderosa del molinero. Esto sucedía tan naturalmente y a través de un proceso sin dolor alguno que yo, que en ocasiones amo tomar entre mis manos el control de la conversación, me sentía feliz de sentarme cerca del saco de grano, a veces por horas, para oír y disfrutar, y aprender como nunca antes lo había hecho a los pies de mis buenos profesores. Aprendí a entender y a hablar el dialecto particular del alemán que estas personas usaban; aprendí a conocer todas sus personalidades con sus lados buenos y malos; aprendí a ver el grano bueno bajo la cáscara, dondequiera que hubiera uno; me familiaricé minuciosamente con los trucos y argumentos usados por los variados enemigos del verdadero luteranismo, y tenía ahora entre mis manos algunas armas poderosas para usar en contra de ellos que me fueron dadas por este viejo teólogo molinero; tomé allí un curso minucioso de posgrado en la aplicación de nuestra doctrina luterana en las nuevas condiciones especiales que estaba enfrentando en mi labor misionera.

Al comienzo aprendí oyendo solamente, pero después de unos pocos meses comencé a unirme a la conversación, haciendo los ejercicios prácticos necesarios bajo la supervisión de mi maestro. En tales ocasiones, después de que los clientes del molino se habían ido, yo le preguntaba al molinero-misionero si mi lenguaje había sido claro y si mis argumentos habían sido entendidos por aquellos a quienes yo estaba intentando dirigirme; y él siempre me decía con absoluta franqueza cuales de mis palabras y frases habían sido "muy gramaticales" para el oyente. Recibí mi diploma al final de mi primer año, después de un debate con el principal enemigo que duró de 7 am hasta las 7 pm con poca interrupción y solo para tomar un vaso de agua, en el cual mi maestro pensó que no necesitaba intervenir (y fue una prueba de su maravilloso tacto que no lo hiciera), pero se restringió a proveer unos pocos testigos luteranos; después del debate, él ofreció la afirmación de que ahora mis oyentes ya me entendían. Sentí más gozo con este diploma que con los dos diplomas en latín que había recibido en otras dos ocasiones.

Entre el molino y la casa de residencia había una cocina vieja, una casucha sin piso, con puertas deterioradas y sin marcos, ventanas cerradas, una pared con la mitad consumida por el fuego. Delante del resto de esta pared colgaba un cable de una viga, en cuyo extremo más bajo colgaba una tetera sobre el fuego, y alrededor del fuego estaba la manada de perros y gatos, vigilando la tetera y disfrutando del calor.

Aquellos quienes tienen el privilegio de conocer los encantos secretos de esta cocina vieja todavía hablan de ella como "la cocina de la bruja". Pero en esa caldera ninguna mazamorra de mendigo burbujea, ni tampoco ningún caldo encantado de bruja. Cada mañana se ponía dentro del caldero nuestra ración diaria de frijoles negros brasileros y tocino ahumado o costillas de cerdo. Y cada mediodía, justo cuando el estómago de uno comenzaba a dejarse oír en un lenguaje inconfundible, la ración estaba deliciosamente lista para ser trasladada del caldero a los platos de los comensales. ¡Ah, cómo me domina esa misma hambre aquí en la hermosa ciudad de New York, entre esta variedad perpleja de cosas buenas para comer, con tan solo pensar en esas comidas de frijoles, el regalo de Dios para Brasil! ¡Y nuestra manera de comer era tan fácil y cómoda! El señor Mertens era solo un inquilino, su familia estaba en su propio "lote rural" a una corta distancia del molino, así que estábamos en una casa sin una mamá. Es así que nunca comimos en una mesa, más aún porque no teníamos una, pero cada uno venía y llenaba su plato cuando estuviera listo. Y cada uno escogía la postura que le gustara más, parado, sentado o reclinado.

Eso me recuerda una pintura que vi en la vieja cocina de la bruja que podría valer un millón si hubiera sido restaurada. Tuvimos un invitado, uno nacido en Leipziger y graduado en nuestro seminario de Porto Alegre, el Rev. Raschke. Un día me ganó sirviéndose la carne y los frijoles. Cuando yo entré a la cocina este hombre pequeño y encorvado se sentó en una banca baja, con el precioso plato de frijoles en sus rodillas. Justo antes de que él se sentara, nuestro querido perrito Wackerlos, con su graciosa nariz bien entrenada en modesta restricción, inmediatamente bajo el borde del plato (una restricción que vino muy naturalmente, puesto que le faltaba la longitud para alcanzar más alto). Detrás de él y sobre él, nuestro perro callejero Gaspodin Brasovitch, largo, flaco y solo medio civilizado, agarró con su hocico bárbaro y de la manera más impropia el borde del plato. Bajo el brazo derecho del señor Raschke nuestra venerable y canosa gata, Mother Puss, se había acercado deleitándose con el olor de los frijoles. Y bajo su brazo izquierdo nuestra bella gatita Narcissa, con por lo menos tres generaciones de cultura en su sangre, disfrutaba el perfume del tocino con su pequeña nariz. Y el señor Raschke, mientras tanto, disfrutaba el momento y sanaba su hombre interior, como lo diría el señor Mertens. Hubo solo una ocasión en mi vida cuando me arrepentí de no tener una cámara lista, y fue en esta ocasión.

La casa ubicada cerca al molino viejo fue el punto de partida de mis viajes a diferentes campos misioneros, de los cuales tuve 17 al comienzo. Porque junto a los trece en la torta de migas, había cuatro más a una distancia de ocho a veinte horas cabalgando. Estas horas equivalen a cerca de cuatro millas cada una. En tiempo de lluvia tomaba mucho más que una hora cabalgando. Durante mi primer año, usé prácticamente dos caballos, puesto que, en promedio, de cinco días de la semana me los pasaba en el camino, generalmente desde la mañana hasta casi la media noche. Después de perder un tercer caballo debido a un suceso desafortunado y sin intención, me quedé con un caballo viejo y huesudo que probablemente era el primer primo de Spark

Plug de las tiras cómicas, lo que me llevó a decidir renunciar a los caballos. Tuve la suerte de conseguir dos mulas "Missouri" finas y grandes, importadas de la República de Uruguay. Eran completamente indomables y tenían un miedo atroz a cualquier hombre que no fuera un entrenador negro nativo. Los domadores de caballos brasileros también estaban temerosos de estos animales grandes y negros, y yo no consentí que las domaran quitándoles la comida hasta que casi murieran, lo cual es una práctica común. Nosotros las amarramos a un vagón de carga de madera en la compañía de otras mulas, y después los muchachos del señor Mertens las montaron por primera vez. Después de esto, las mulas estuvieron al servicio de la misión, aunque esto significó poner mi vida en riesgo cada vez que las montaba, pues aún eran animales semidomados. Pero después que llegaron a conocerme, y después que desarrollé un sistema para relacionarme con ellas, tuve dos bestias de carga a las que no se las podía matar, y no las habría cambiado ni por la mejor media docena de caballos de Kentucky.

Estos viajes a lomo de mula fueron especialmente interesantes, lo que no quiere decir, sin embargo, que fueran agradables. Poco después de la llegada de las mulas, yo también me mudé a la casa parroquial, aunque todavía faltaba terminarse la mitad. Desde allí fui llamado un día para bautizar a un pequeño niño en un lugar a cinco millas de distancia. No había hoyos de barro en el camino, sino que todo el camino era un solo hoyo de barro hasta la rodilla. Esto quería decir que iba a montar la mula todo el camino. Después del bautismo, la madre del niño pidió tomar la comunión. Yo no había traído vino y no había ningún lugar donde encontrarlo cerca de la casa parroquial. Tampoco había nadie a quien mandar a conseguirlo, o ningún caballo para que alguien cabalgara. Entonces la única cosa que me quedaba era cabalgar de regreso y regresar con los elementos necesarios. Cuando me fui de nuevo de esa casa después de la comunión, el sol ya estaba ocultándose. Pero ya se había anunciado una boda para la tarde. Para evitar desilusiones, yo había dejado una nota para los contrayentes diciendo que se dirigieran a la casa de los padres de la novia una vez hubiera terminado el matrimonio civil, prometiéndoles llegar allí tan pronto como pudiera. Para ahorrarme una milla de caminos malos, tomé un sendero nuevo que todavía no había sido usado lo suficiente como para convertirse en barro hasta la rodilla. La noche era oscura. Ese sendero, cerrado arriba por el ramaje verde, era tan oscuro como un túnel de piedra sólida. Solo por el salpicar de las patas de la mula, podía saber que todavía estábamos en el sendero. Yo iba muy alerta, pues esperaba que en cualquier momento mi cráneo o mis ojos fueran golpeados por una de las inmensas ramas. Y por experiencia, sabía que cualquier ruido inusual, como el chasquido de un junco quebrado, podía hacer que mi joven y asustada mula comenzara a correr para salvar su vida. Lo peor que pasó en un largo tiempo fue que una rama tumbó mi sombrero y tuve que buscarlo en la oscuridad. Y de este modo cabalgué y cabalgué y cabalgué. Algunas cosas se expanden por el calor, pero las millas se expanden por la oscuridad. De repente, mi mula se paró en sus patas traseras girando en ellas como trompo. No pude hacer nada para pararla. Así que hice la segunda mejor cosa que podía hacer:

me senté en la montura y esperé, sabiendo que no era posible que la mula gire toda la noche. Y no lo hizo. Cuando paró, me desenredé de las enredaderas y me bajé. Un árbol estaba caído en la mitad del sendero. Yo pensé que con seguridad ya había un sendero de emergencia alrededor de esta obstrucción y traté de conducir a mi mula hacia él. El animal rehusó a ser conducido en la oscuridad. La até a un retoño de árbol y encontré el sendero de emergencia cayéndome en el barro y llenando mis botas de barro. Aun así, estuve contento con esa situación. Regresé a la mula, me monté y me acerqué [al sendero]. Pero cuando llegué allí, no sabía absolutamente nada sobre la dirección de la cual había venido. Tampoco sobre la dirección en la cual estaba yendo. Por un momento me senté y lo pensé. Sin resultados. Volví a pensarlo más detenidamente. Tampoco obtuve ningún resultado. Lo volví a pensar más cuidadosamente. Resultados. Un rayo de luz en esa temible oscuridad: "Solo puede ser incorrecto de una manera, entonces la otra debe ser la correcta". Seguí cabalgando. Y cabalgué, y cabalgué, y cabalgué, y todavía cabalgué. Entonces vino el primer rayo de luz física. Me encontraba en un camino más ancho y abierto arriba. Había llegado. Lo reconocí por un tronco inmenso al lado del camino que estaba de regreso al lugar donde había visto el atardecer. ¿Qué podía hacer sino respirar aire profundamente y relajarme y continuar cabalgando hasta la casa parroquial? A su debido tiempo, un poco antes de la medianoche, llegué a la casa de la novia, encontré al futuro esposo durmiendo profundamente debido al alcohol consumido, y llevé a cabo la ceremonia matrimonial en medio de interrupciones por parte de los invitados borrachos.

En otra ocasión, había comprado un número de mapas para mis escuelas en Ijuhy. Para asegurarme de que llegarían secos a casa, los envolví en mi abrigo impermeable y los envié con un conductor. Era un buen día soleado de invierno. Intenté tomar una ruta indirecta, incrementando la distancia en 20 horas. Pero quería cabalgar esta distancia sin ninguna parada y en la noche, para no perder la hora de instrucción de catecismo en casa. Hacia el anochecer comenzó a lloviznar y entre más oscuro se puso, más fuerte llovía, y más frío se puso. ¡Y pobre de mí que solo vestía un traje de montar! Cuando eran casi las siete en punto, nosotros, es decir, la mula y yo, nos caímos en una cuneta. Siempre he sostenido que esto fue intencional por parte de la mula. Pero no quería arriesgarme de nuevo. Con la iluminación momentánea de un rayo, escogí un arbusto de espinas bajo el cual buscar refugio. No es que estuviera lloviendo menos allí, sino que hay cierta sensación de protección bajo un arbusto, en medio de la llanura plana con lluvia y relámpagos y truenos. Para no cansarme, me paré primero en una pierna y después cambié a la otra. La mula hizo casi lo mismo. Después de casi doce horas en este cambio alternado, llegó el alba y la lluvia se redujo y finalmente dejó de llover. El sol caliente empezó a hacer su trabajo de secar mis ropas mojadas, y después de diez horas en la montura llegué a casa, sin sentir el temor de ser regañado por haber mojado mi ropa buena. Incluso encontré una vara de hierro en el camino, la recogí y la devolví al conductor que la había perdido, lo cual lo hizo muy feliz.

Tenía trece estaciones de predicación en mis alrededores inmediatos, cuando ocho ya eran mucho. Existían (junto con el número de escuelas de la Iglesia Unida) debido al hecho de que a la gente se le había ordenado con mano de hierro desde arriba cuando todavía estaban en Rusia, y por supuesto sabían tan poco sobre la administración práctica de las congregaciones como de la doctrina. Además, había falta de caminos en este asentamiento. Las paredes de bosque ininterrumpido se dividieron en tres congregaciones largas y estrechas, lo cual debió haber sido una sola de forma casi cuadrada. Pronto me di cuenta de que, por predicar en tantos lugares, solamente estaba desperdiciando mi fortaleza física y mental. Como regla, yo sólo podía tener una audiencia una vez cada cuatro o seis meses, contando los domingos lluviosos, lo cual no era mucho mejor que lo que los pastores en Rusia habían estado haciendo. Y entre mis visitas escasas y retiradas, la buena semilla de la Palabra fácilmente podía ser cubierta por la cizaña de algunos falsos profetas, que tenían su oportunidad una o dos veces a la semana.

En la vieja "cocina de la bruja", pronto nos encontramos ocupados deliberando sobre las maneras y medios para alcanzar una mayor organización práctica en la totalidad de la iglesia luterana dentro de la torta de migas de Guarany. La fundación de una congregación grande y central con sus oficinas centrales en la casa parroquial o cerca, que fueran construidas por el Sínodo y la adición gradual de muchas más congregaciones pequeñas en los alrededores, probablemente cerca de cuatro, parecía ser la cosa más natural a la que pudiéramos aspirar. El único paso práctico que yo podía tomar mientras vivía en el viejo molino era hacer una junta de presidentes de las llamadas 13 congregaciones para ganar su consentimiento y enlistar su interés en este plan. Mientras que esto no pudo haber sido totalmente en vano, no puedo decir que trajo mucho progreso.

Desde el momento en que tomé como residencia la casa parroquial medio terminada, estuve en la posición de avanzar con otras medidas. La primera fue organizar lo que nosotros llamábamos la noche escolar. Los hombres jóvenes, más progresivos, de las diferentes "congregaciones" eran invitados a reunirse cada viernes en la noche en el estudio del pastor. Nosotros estudiábamos el alemán leyendo, deletreando, también la gramática y algo de portugués. Teníamos algunos minutos para la rutina parlamentaria, para acostumbrarnos a presidentes, secretarias, llamados de asistencia, mociones, formulación de preguntas y cosas por el estilo, que eran ideas bastante nuevas para la mayoría de los miembros. También, comencé la lectura de una serie de historias de Alfred Ira sobre algunos de los problemas de la vida congregacional tratados de una manera magistral. Para asegurar la asistencia y la atención de todos los miembros lo más posible, bebíamos nuestro té brasilero durante estas lecturas.

Este té consiste en las hojas y ramitas pulverizadas del mate sudamericano o té de Paraguay.[1] Este té, el cual es un sustituto espléndido del té oriental cuando se bebe

1 Pastor Albert aquí refiere al cimarrón, una bebida tradicional del sur de Brasil y otros países de América del Sur. Es preparada con una infusión de yerba mate molida, servada con agua caliente en una calabaza y consumida por medio de una bombilla. Se trata de

como una decocción suave, usualmente se bebe en Sudamérica de una forma mucho más fuerte. Una calabaza pequeña u otro recipiente apropiado se llena con el polvo del té, dejando espacio en un lado para insertar una bombilla de plata con una especie de colador al final. Entonces el espacio de aire se llena con agua casi hirviendo. El resultado de la fuerte cocción se succiona con bombilla de plata. El anfitrión toma la primera servida, después sirve a los demás invitados. El sabor de la bebida es bastante amargo para los nuevos asistentes, y el hecho de que muchas personas succionan del mismo objeto puede ser visto por el norteamericano corriente como una manera escondida de cometer suicidio. Pero en muchas partes de Sudamérica este es un rito sagrado de hospitalidad, y una vez que uno se haya acostumbrado al sabor y esté cautivado por el hábito y el poder estimulante de la bebida, sé que ninguna otra bebida en el mundo puede brindar la misma medida de sociabilidad democrática como esta. No estoy proponiendo su introducción al mundo civilizado, pues pienso que contiene mucho ácido tánico (11 por ciento) para ser saludable. Pero nosotros lo utilizamos en nuestras reuniones con un propósito, y estoy seguro que esta bebida aseguró el éxito de nuestras conversaciones. El propósito principal de la escuela era conocernos los unos a los otros y tener la oportunidad para hablar sobre el plan de organización. Tuvimos éxito. Los antiguos asistentes de la escuela nocturna no solamente son los miembros más activos y comprensivos de nuestras reestructuradas congregaciones, sino que también algunos de ellos están prestando servicio como presidentes y secretarios.

Lo siguiente que resolvimos fue el problema del correo y también comenzamos nuestra biblioteca circulante. Aún después de la terminación del nuevo pedazo del ferrocarril ("mi ferrocarril"), la casa parroquial estaba a once horas de camino de la estación más cercana, a cuatro horas de la oficina del correo gubernamental, y a tres horas del teléfono más cercano. Con frecuencia, mi correo hacía una vuelta peligrosa de ida y vuelta antes de encontrarme. Y si hay una cosa en el mundo que me altere los nervios es una oficina de correos negligente. Así que era totalmente natural para mi llevar a cabo un plan modelo de un sistema de correo privado, el cual consistía en traernos nuestro correo directamente de la oficina de correos una vez por semana. Después de varias experiencias, las cuales describí en el Atlantic Monthly (revista norteamericana) en ese tiempo, el correo llegó a ser, como debería ser, algo sagrado y que nos alegraba, y por años había estado llegando a la casa parroquial cada viernes en la noche, con sol o lluvia, para ser distribuido a todas las congregaciones el sábado o el domingo en la mañana. Al comienzo, los hombres de la escuela nocturna hicieron la distribución, después los maestros. Y ahora teníamos una organización a la cual podíamos confiar la distribución exitosa de publicaciones y libros en los hogares, y después, llevar a cabo varias actividades sirviendo a una publicidad digna para nuestra

una bebida de gran importancia cultural, cuyo ritual de preparación y consumo simboliza tradición y compañerismo.

iglesia y la escuela. A pesar de las medidas entorpecedoras de la guerra, tuvimos éxito en distribuir un buen número de publicaciones. Y los libros de la biblioteca circulante estaban casi siempre prestados a la comunidad. Supe de un número de personas jóvenes quienes, por no haber tenido la oportunidad de ir a la escuela durante su niñez, ahora habían aprendido a leer muy bien por medio de esta biblioteca y no tenían miedo de abordar los libros densos. Y los padres que no sabían leer, ahora podían disfrutar de literatura maravillosa oyendo a sus hijos leer.

Pero como la necesidad de escuelas reales era la mayor necesidad de todas, la Conferencia de Maestros fue la piedra angular de toda nuestra labor organizacional. Un número pequeño de "maestros" habían venido de Rusia y permanecieron en su oficio siendo respetados como una reliquia familiar por las congregaciones, tanto como les fuera posible. Estos maestros no sabían nada de buenos métodos de enseñanza y su mayor ayuda era dar con una vara a los estudiantes. Con el transcurso de los años, el abastecimiento de esta valiosa clase de humanidad se terminó. Nosotros lamentamos el hecho de que el Sínodo no tuviera maestros para llenar los puestos vacantes. Pero no perdimos mucho tiempo lamentándonos. Un número de hombres jóvenes que sabían leer y escribir fueron escogidos. La mayoría de ellos no tuvo educación escolar en su adolescencia. Pero tenían la buena disposición de recuperar el tiempo perdido lo más que pudieran. Y yo estuve más que dispuesto a darles una oportunidad. Nos reuníamos en conferencia en la casa parroquial cada sábado. Allí dimos nuestros primeros pasos, dialogando sobre las cosas que un niño debe aprender las primeras semanas y meses de la vida escolar. Esto era necesario, no solo para mostrar a los hombres cómo impartir este conocimiento a los niños, sino también porque yo había descubierto que ellos lo necesitaban para su propio bien. De este modo, fuimos sorprendidos un día al saber que uno de nuestros hombres ancianos, quien había enseñado en la escuela por varios años, no sabía que toda oración debe comenzar con mayúscula. Después de este descubrimiento, no debería haberme sorprendido en absoluto encontrarlo escribiendo su propio nombre "wlAdislaW steinbRennEr". Este no fue el único descubrimiento hecho. Pero pronto mostramos progreso. El trabajo escolar comenzó a mover una pulsación sana donde antes había sido solo tropezones. Los padres comenzaron a parar sus orejas. Los visitantes ocasionales de las escuelas notaron que el maestro nunca se sentaba detrás del escritorio (es decir, la dura banca de madera detrás del escritorio), sino que estaba de pie cada minuto del día escolar. También se sorprendieron de que el maestro muy rara vez o nunca utilizara la vara excepto para señalar algo. Los sorprendió aún más, que los niños estuvieran aprendiendo más a pesar de esta negación del castigo físico, como nunca antes lo habían soñado posible. Estuvieron fascinados cuando sus muchachos y muchachas llevaban a casa libros de historias maravillosas y los leían a sus padres casi con la misma fluidez e inteligencia del maestro o del pastor. Pero se alcanzó el límite cuando ellos asistieron a los exámenes públicos y vieron a sus propios hijos, entre otras cosas, deletrear las palabras más difíciles del idioma alemán sin libros y con gran autoconfianza.

¿Quién ha experimentado esto en Rusia, aunque sea en sueños? Y también palabras en portugués. Y ellos leían y traducían portugués sin obstáculo alguno. El antiguo argumento de los hombres viejos y sabios comenzó a perder su fuerza: "yo no puedo leer ni escribir y he venido desde Rusia hasta Brasil; no veo por qué mis hijos deben saber más que yo". Los celos sanos comenzaron a crecer entre los padres: los hijos de mi vecino no pueden leer tan bien como los míos; y, además, mis propios hijos no deben asistir menos a la escuela que los de mi vecino. Se hizo necesario recordar a los padres que no debían mandar a sus hijos a la escuela si estaban muy pequeños. El año pasado seis familias de una congregación estaban mandando treinta niños a la escuela. Toda la congregación de 28 miembros estaba enviando 72 niños. Y tenía que ser un día muy lluvioso para que la asistencia no estuviera por encima de sesenta. Algunas veces, en días lluviosos, el maestro o maestra se quedaba en casa, pensando que tendría un día de descanso. Pero era una tontería pensarlo, porque los niños iban a buscar a sus maestros a sus casas para llevarlos a la escuela. Los padres se quejaban con el pastor de que ellos no podían tener a sus hijos en casa cuando los necesitaban. De más está decir que hubo algunos padres, y unos pocos niños, que no se unieron a esta ola general de entusiasmo escolar.

Y entonces vinieron nuestros coros. Dios envió a un hombre a la casa parroquial, que de otra manera no hubiera servido para nada, pero que amaba la música y estaba entrenado y dotado de una voz por la gracia de Dios. Por varios años él contuvo sus malas inclinaciones, como el alcoholismo, entre otras, a tal extremo que le permitió conducir e inspirar nuestros coros, hasta que años más tarde, el tiempo del pastor permitió que él se hiciera cargo de esta labor. En el transcurso de cerca de seis años, nuestros siete distintos coros cantaron cientos de las composiciones corales del mundo, la coral de La Pasión según San Mateo de Bach, entre otras. Los cantantes siempre estaban llenos de entusiasmo y casi nunca se daban cuenta de la labor difícil y espléndida que estaban haciendo. Nosotros nunca nos olvidamos de la meta fundamental que teníamos, la de promover la organización de las congregaciones mediante los coros. Hicimos esto al liderar a la gente a nuestros servicios, al entrenar las congregaciones en el canto de nuestros antiguos corales luteranos de la manera original, y al utilizar los ensayos para llevar a cabo discusiones fructíferas sobre los problemas congregacionales. Un importante éxito fue el que tuvimos excluyendo los himnos del estilo Moody-Sankey, los cuales fueron traídos con traducciones alemanas abominables y eran apreciados por sus melodías que cosquilleaban los oídos y sus ritmos que inspiraban el movimiento de los pies.[2]

2 David Sankey (28 de agosto do 1840–13 de agosto de 1908) fue un cantor y compositor de música góspel norteamericano, conocido por su larga colaboración con Dwight L. Moody (5 de febrero de 1837–22 de diciembre de 1899), un evangelista norteamericano. Juntos, ellos realizaran un ciclo de campañas de avivamiento religioso en los Estados Unidos y Gran Bretaña durante las últimas décadas del siglo XIX. Los himnos cantados

Estos resultados no fueron logrados sin conflictos. Debo mencionar solo los más importantes y de manera breve. Hubo una lucha en contra del patriotismo local. Todos estaban dispuestos a unirse a congregaciones más grandes para estar seguros. Pero todos querían que todos los demás vinieran a ellos todo el tiempo. "¡Debe ser en nuestra calle, en nuestra escuela!". Fue en contra de este enemigo que nuestros coros probaron ser un arma poderosa. Después hubo un conflicto en contra de los pietistas y los autoproclamados predicadores, especialmente los así llamados "Brethren" o hermanos (Gemeinschaftsbrüder), quienes eran tan santos en sus propios ojos al punto de estar en peligro de volar al cielo en sus propias ropas de trabajo. Ellos estaban lanzando la red de Cristo con toda su fuerza, pero desafortunadamente en la dirección equivocada. La mayoría de ellos se volvieron bautistas y después pensadores libres. Hubo desacuerdos con aquellos quienes tarde o temprano se manifestaron como pensadores libres. Estos fueron, en su mayoría, de muchas de las "congregaciones" más pequeñas, y en algunos casos la minoría luterana perdió la propiedad de sus iglesias. En otros casos, la propiedad tuvo que venderse y dividir el dinero. En tales casos, la regla fue culpar al pastor por haber causado las discordias. En todos los casos, esta culpa fue del pastor. Era la Palabra de Dios en contra de la cual ellos estaban peleando, y fue Dios quien otorgó la victoria de su espada en todos los casos, aunque no siempre de la misma manera. Su poder divino fue siempre tan explícitamente manifestado como para ser sentido por el pastor o como para que cualquiera de los miembros se jactara de ello. Y Dios no solo causó que las tormentas se detuvieran y que los rayos del sol regresaran al tiempo preciso, sino que también hizo que los verdaderos luteranos, un número pequeño, pero no como para ser despreciado, viera que no había otro camino a la paz que no fuera mediante la batalla y el conflicto.

Y no hay que decirle al lector que la vida personal del pastor no fue siempre un camino sembrado de rosas. Pero quiero mencionar algunos detalles, no para ponerme en un pedestal, sino para justificar el título "Abriendo fronteras para Cristo en las selvas de Brasil". En primer lugar, no es incorrecto mencionar el lado mental de la dificultad. Me temo que el lector difícilmente pueda imaginar lo que significa para un hombre cuya mente y alma se han desarrollado en la apreciación de todo lo bueno, noble y lleno de contenido intelectual, desarrollado por lo que para él siempre parecerá un hogar excepcional, por un buen maestro y pastor, por casi una veintena de profesores que en su mayoría eran hombres excelentes, desarrollado en todas las cosas buenas durante más de veinte años... digo, difícilmente pueda imaginar lo que significa para tal persona ser repentinamente abandonado en la naturaleza salvaje del sur de Brasil, entre personas cuyas cualidades más destacadas están el analfabetismo, la embriaguez, la superficialidad y la mayor grosería en el lenguaje y las costumbres.

---

en esas campañas eran caracterizados por un foco en conversión emocional, melodías simples y fáciles de cantar y participación de la congregación.

Antes de que recibiera mi llamado para Brasil, había pasado casi un año entre los vagabundos, los atorrantes de frutas, y otros patoteros de nuestro propio salvaje oeste. El lector me perdonará si no explico aquí cómo llegué a parar en compañía de tales. Ahora sé lo que no sabía en ese entonces, de que era otra de las escuelas de Dios para mi obra misionera en Brasil. Solo quiero decir que estos vagabundos no pueden estar a la altura de algunos de mis rusos alemanes en la aspereza de su idioma. En algunas ocasiones me sentí agradecido de que no fue mi suerte haber traído a una muchacha americana dentro de esta atmósfera, aunque no quiero decir con esto que una verdadera muchacha leal americana, si hubiera sido ubicada en tal atmósfera por la voluntad de Dios, no hubiera podido ser perfectamente feliz al servicio de Dios allí. Y en caso de que se me olvide el lado positivo, quiero recordarme a mí mismo y al lector que este triste páramo de analfabetismo y vulgaridad tuvo para mí un agradable oasis en la persona del Sr. Mertens, quien fue realmente mi única "compañía" durante mi primer uno y dos años.

Ya les he dado algunos ejemplos de lo que los muchos viajes crueles significaron y a los cuales un misionero está sujeto en su labor. Quiero recurrir a este tema una vez más con toda seriedad, sin quitar ninguna de las dificultades cuando muestro el lado humorístico. Nunca había sentido mucho estos viajes largos y crueles como un sacrificio de mi parte, sino que lo sentía como una pérdida inadmisible de fuerzas que le pertenecían a Dios. Los poderes del misionero para el cumplimiento eficiente de sus múltiples tareas, sus poderes corporales, su potencia de nervios, la frescura de su mentalidad, son todos inexcusablemente limitados por los golpes que se da en la silla de montar hora tras hora. Una vez, durante una hora débil en uno de estos viajes, conté los pasos de mi mula en un minuto y los multipliqué por el número de minutos que hay en diez horas de un viaje que tenía que hacer con frecuencia: un total de noventa mil sacudidas. Sería una estupidez creer que un ser humano podría predicar tan potentemente, o instruir muy bien, o estar muy atento a las oportunidades para realizar el trabajo pastoral con individuos como debería después de tantas sacudidas de arriba abajo, como lo estaría si los baches del camino hubieran sido, en su mayor parte, absorbidos por un buen conjunto de resortes de carruaje. Y a esto se reduce finalmente: a la pérdida grande de los poderes del misionero, derramados en el camino, por la falta de un buen conjunto de resortes de carruajes en el cual montarse. Y no podemos comprar carruajes en Brasil, y el misionero individual no puede importarlos, y la junta de misiones no tiene dinero para enviarlos, o alguna otra cosa anda mal en alguna parte. El misionero no sabe dónde está el obstáculo realmente. Pero esto quebranta el corazón del misionero, no porque su viejo esqueleto esté sufriendo, sino porque la obra del Señor no es llevada a cabo como se debería.

Si se me perdona por escribir unas pocas palabras más sobre un tema algo doloroso, me gustaría llamar la atención a la parte más dura de tal viaje cruel. Es el regreso a casa en la total oscuridad, en medio de un aguacero, en caminos donde cada paso puede traer la muerte. No quiero decir la muerte por los animales salvajes de la región.

Nunca me he encontrado con un animal peligroso, tampoco he sido atacado por asaltantes. Me refiero a los peligros de partirse el cráneo o la nuca al chocar con una rama colgante, el peligro de cortarse la garganta con un junco partido, el peligro de deslizarse, caerse, ser arrastrado por el animal que uno está cabalgando hasta morir. No estoy hablando de fantasías. Me he salvado milagrosamente muchas veces de todos estos peligros y de otros. Tampoco estoy intentando ganarme la simpatía de los lectores. He sido tan feliz en mi trabajo cada día de estos ocho años que no sabría qué hacer con tal simpatía, si la tuviera. Solo quiero decir lo que comencé a decir al principio, que estos viajes en la oscuridad durante horas, junto con la incertidumbre peligrosa colgando sobre la cabeza, son la parte más dura de nuestra vida cruel en la silla de montar, y una hora de esto siempre pareció desgarrar mis nervios más que cinco horas de la luz del día, o sin lluvia, o en caminos buenos y nivelados. Y también quiero señalar que, en la mayoría de los casos, donde el camino es lo suficientemente ancho como para una carreta o carro, un carruaje con una lámpara atada eliminaría la mayor parte de este estrés nervioso.

Mi vida hogareña, también, tenía suficiente dificultad como para que fuera aburrida e insípida. En un párrafo anterior me referí a nuestra manera de vivir en el molino viejo. Más adelante, en la casa parroquial, tuve más la sensación de vivir en mi propio hogar, pero tuve que llevarme bien por algunos pocos años con sirvientes masculinos de distintas clases, quienes también cocinaban de distintas maneras. Uno de ellos tenía pasión por las sopas, preparaba un queso excelente, creía firmemente que mi vaca estaba embrujada, y tenía el hábito de secar sus medias en la lata de café. Después tuve un cocinero que sabía cocinar, pero tenía otras fallas como, por ejemplo, apropiarse del dinero que estaba en la gaveta, lo cual no era mucho, puesto que la gaveta del dinero de un misionero está casi siempre vacía.

Los representantes del Sínodo tuvieron las mejores intenciones con la casa parroquial. Un edificio grande de dos pisos con dieciséis habitaciones, diseñado para alojar a dos misioneros, con el número más grande de ventanas francesas que yo haya visto en una casa de ese tamaño. Con la excepción de mi estudio, las ventanas estuvieron sin vidrio durante la guerra, y por algún tiempo después de terminada la casa. Tampoco había contraventanas. En Brasil llueve bastante. En ocasiones, teníamos la sensación de que llovía todo el tiempo. Y con cada lluvia el agua caía del cielorraso del lado donde estuviera soplando el viento. En algunas lluvias caía agua por los cuatro lados de la casa. Pero fuimos entrenados, como la tripulación de un barco, a almacenar todos los bienes movibles en el lado seco de la casa. Y cuando el viento cambiaba, almacenábamos todo en el lado contrario de la casa. Y algunas veces nos encontrábamos sentados en el lado protegido y no nos dábamos cuenta de que la lluvia estaba entrando en el otro lado y después encontrábamos algunos libros arruinados o una cama mojada completamente o incluso cubierta con una capa de arcilla de barro proveniente de la pared sin terminar. Esto, también, era fuerte para los nervios. Pero puedo decir que siempre intenté encontrar el lado cómico. Uno de esos lados cómicos fue que el piso era absolutamente a prueba de agua. Tuvimos que taladrar huecos en él para sacar el agua. Pero después de que tuve una esposa, y antes de que tuviera la idea de los huecos en el piso, y cada vez que habíamos almacenado las cosas en el lado seco de la casa, antes de que el viento tuviera la oportunidad de girar, nos agarrábamos de las manos y bailábamos con los pies descalzos en el mar de los pisos del estudio y del comedor. Ese era el lado cómico, pero en ocasiones tenía mis dudas sobre si la mayoría de las mujeres hubieran pensado que esto era cómico. Pero después de todo, tenía un hogar y fue siempre un verdadero hogar para mí. Y después de ocho años de construcción, la casa parroquial estuvo casi terminada y ahora la lluvia rara vez se entraba en los cuartos y casi nunca volvieron a mojar las camas.

Ya había dado la noticia de que después de algunos años de soltería ya había encontrado una mamá para mi hogar. En esos cuatro años de soledad, algunas veces me preocupaba de cómo alguna mujer podría encontrarme en los bosques brasileros para casarse conmigo. Esta preocupación, como todas las preocupaciones, fue innecesaria. Justo en el tiempo preciso, Dios me dio la provisión, sin ninguna ayuda de mi parte, para que la muchacha más querida (por mí) de todo el mundo, se convirtiera en la vecina de mi parroquia. Muy naturalmente, el enamoramiento creció rápidamente. Cuando estuvimos comprometidos, aparecieron un número de delegaciones por parte de los miembros de las congregaciones demandando que se rompiera el compromiso, porque ellos no intentarían aceptar a una muchacha de la congregación como esposa de su pastor. Y también vinieron delegaciones de personas que no eran miembros de las iglesias demandando que continuáramos con el compromiso, de lo contrario nos involucrarían en un escándalo periodístico. Las dos distintas delegaciones no alteraron el transcurso de la historia en lo más mínimo.

Ninguno de los dos teníamos dinero para la tal llamada boda. En la noche de nuestro matrimonio legal celebramos solos. Cinco días más tarde, cabalgamos juntos a Ijuhy, donde nos casamos en una iglesia y esta es la fecha a la cual llamamos nuestro día oficial de boda. Y una boda simple, pero hermosa, fue preparada para nosotros por el reverendo Müller y su esposa, y el maestro Naumann y su esposa. Entre los invitados estuvieron varios pastores y maestros que estaban de camino a una conferencia. También nos convencieron de viajar junto con ellos a la conferencia. A nuestro regreso, tomamos prestado el carruaje del reverendo Müller para las últimas cien millas. Estando en Brasil, no era una sorpresa que dobláramos el eje delantero cuando se cruzaba el primer río. El siguiente incidente fue que mis mulas caminaron hacia el centro de una laguna grande, entonces se pararon y me miraron como diciendo: "ven y sácanos de aquí si nos necesitas". Lo cual yo hice. Después, nos estancamos en barro duro hasta los ejes en uno de los ríos, las mulas jalaron como si fueran sesenta y ambos balancines se quebraron como palillos de dientes. Creo que las mulas hicieron esto intencionalmente. En todos los eventos fuimos forzados a bajarnos a levantar el carruaje con el barro hasta las rodillas. Y después, una de esas lluvias reales brasileras comenzó a caer y continuó hasta que llegamos a casa. Ese fue nuestro viaje de luna de miel. Después de esto, hemos vivido felices por siempre.

Si tuviera el espacio, me gustaría escribir una cosa o dos sobre esa maravillosa mujer, quien es mi esposa. Pero las cosas más importantes estarán grabadas en el último capítulo del libro de Proverbios. Quiero agregar que ella es ruso-alemana de nacimiento, una brasilera por adopción desde que tuvo once años, y una americana por simpatía y por matrimonio. No fue a la escuela, pero es una lectora maravillosa. En sus días de confirmación, e incluso después, memorizó todo el catecismo sinódico, incluyendo la mayor parte de la introducción de Lutero. En su niñez, caminaba 14 millas de ida y 14 millas de vuelta ese mismo día, en la lluvia y descalza, por supuesto, para oír uno de los conciertos de nuestro coro. Como madre, es una de las personas que mejor conoce en cuanto a la educación científica de los hijos. Sé que me perdonarán por revelar tanto de la historia familiar, porque mujeres buenas e interesadas me han preguntado: "¿Tienes una buena esposa?".

También nos han hecho otras preguntas de las que yo debería responder una o dos aquí. "¿Usan anillos de boda en Brasil?". Sí usamos. Por lo menos las personas que tienen el dinero para comprarlos. Nosotros no teníamos el dinero en ese tiempo. Más adelante planeamos comprarlos en Tiffany en New York, como una dulce revancha. Y lo hicimos. Son los usuales anillos matrimoniales y contienen la inscripción: "Urwahnfried—1918". Nada más, pero eso es todo un volumen. Urwahnfried es una palabra compuesta de antiguas raíces alemanas y significa en español moderno "plenitud". O, más explícitamente, "el lugar donde mi batalla por los ideales más altos y amplios de la vida finalizaron en la paz de la victoria". Urwahnfried es el nombre de nuestra casa parroquial en Guarany. También es el nombre de nuestra estación privada de correo, la cual es muy importante, pues mucho de nuestro correo iba en el pasado a un pueblo pequeño llamado Quarahy, en la frontera con la República de Uruguay. Desde la adopción de nuestro propio nombre, no he conocido un caso de correo desaparecido.

Nos preguntaron si hay médicos y enfermeras y parteras en Brasil. Creo que el pequeño Siegfried plantea estas preguntas, el niño alegre del bosque, con sus ojos vivaces, que ignora la enorme desgracia que supone haber nacido en la selva primigenia sin médico ni enfermera. Nuestro doctor más cercano estaba a 60 millas de distancia, lo que significaba de 30 a 60 horas ida y vuelta, dependiendo del clima. Tenemos que darle crédito a este hombre por no habernos dado ningún problema o preocupación en todos estos años. Puesto que cuando lo necesitábamos, no podíamos llegar a él. Y cuando podíamos llegar a él, no lo necesitábamos. Y traerlo a nosotros nos hubiera costado un mes de salario. Había demasiadas parteras en nuestra área de Guarany, pero solo una con entrenamiento o que supiera leer. Algunas del resto traían con ellas una noche completa de ignorancia y superstición medieval. Solo para mencionar un caso que será suficiente para hacer temblar a los americanos: una de las parteras más ocupadas ponía a los bebés recién nacidos afuera de la casa en el piso frío prácticamente sin envolverlo por cerca de una hora para dar a los espíritus malignos la oportunidad de evaporarse. Nosotros preferimos, por razones que nos parecieron valederas, darle la bienvenida nosotros mismos a nuestro pequeño Siegfried. En todas las cosas esenciales, él recibió la misma recepción que hubiera disfrutado en un buen hospital, y Dios hizo el resto. Seríamos deshonestos si dijéramos que lo hubiéramos deseado de otra manera.

En cuanto a mi propia salud, contraje una hemorragia estomacal desde 1916, como consecuencia de los largos y crueles viajes cabalgando. Debo mencionar que, en los tiempos de más debilidad, estando en peligro de perder el sentido a cada segundo, fui forzado a permanecer de pie y llevar a cabo una ceremonia matrimonial. A pesar de esto y de otras cosas, supe estar sano. Pero en 1922 sufrí cuatro recaídas, generalmente a una distancia de entre ocho y diez horas de casa, sin otra forma de llegar que a caballo (o al menos no había otra mejor). Cada ataque me dejó al borde de la muerte y me mantuvo en un estado de extrema debilidad durante un mes o más. Cuando recibí el permiso para tomarme una licencia de un año, había tenido un ataque, y cuando el dinero llegó después de 8 a 9 meses, los otros tres ataques ya habían terminado. Fui a un buen hospital en Alemania y después de una semana de exámenes fui gratamente sorprendido al oír que no existía ninguna huella de defecto alguno en mi estómago. Como no existía ninguna duda de la realidad de las hemorragias, los médicos del hospital parecieron incapaces de explicar el caso con sus teorías. Para mí fue fácil, porque creo en milagros. Los médicos hubieran disfrutado mucho haberme operado al punto de querer reservar la operación para una posible y próxima aparición, lo cual decliné cortésmente.

En conclusión, de esta corta historia de ocho años de dificultades abriendo fronteras para Cristo en las selvas de Brasil, siento que no debería omitir una palabra de Cristo que todo misionero conoce y cree y valora. Está en Marcos 10:29–30: "Respondió Jesús y dijo: De cierto os digo que no hay ninguno que haya dejado casa, o hermanos, o hermanas, o padre, o madre, o mujer, o hijos, o tierras, por causa de mí y del evangelio, que no reciba cien veces más ahora en este tiempo; casas, hermanos, hermanas, madres, hijos, y tierras, con persecuciones; y en el siglo venidero la vida eterna".

No puedo expresar lo mucho que me reconforta volver a disfrutar plenamente de las múltiples bendiciones de la civilización durante mi estancia en Alemania y Estados Unidos, ni lo agradecido que estoy por toda la amabilidad que me han demostrado los hermanos a ambos lados del Atlántico. Pero no hay lugar como Urwahnfried y no hay sustituto alguno para la bendición especial de Dios cuando se está en el campo misionero. El anhelo de mi corazón y mi oración diaria es volver al trabajo poco después de que estas páginas se publiquen, allí donde ya he elegido mi sepultura. Lo único más satisfactorio y bendito que luchar por Cristo es seguir luchando por Cristo.

Albert Lehenbauer, ca. 1942

Albert and Helena [Priebe] Lehenbauer, ca. 1918.

Albert e Helena [Priebe] Lehenbauer, ca. 1918.

Albert y Helena [Priebe] Lehenbauer, ca. 1918.

Albert and Helena Lehenbauer with son Siegfried, ca. 1922.

Albert e Helena Lehenbauer com o filho Siegfried, ca. 1922.

Albert y Helena Lehenbauer con su hijo Siegfried, ca. 1922.

Albert Lehenbauer (then missionary to Guarany and vice president of Seminário Concórdia, Porto Alegre, Brazil) surveys the "Old Colony" on the border between Brazil and Argentina, ca. 1928–37.

Albert Lehenbauer (então missionário em Guarany e vice- presidente do Seminário Concórdia, Porto Alegre, Brasil) observando a "Antiga Colônia" na fronteira entre o Brasil e a Argentina, ca. 1928–37.

Albert Lehenbauer (entonces misionero en Guarany y vicepresidente del Seminário Concórdia, Porto Alegre, Brasil) inspeccionando la "Vieja Colonia" en la frontera entre Brasil y Argentina, ca. 1928–37.

Urwahnfried